THE

TRUE CRIME

QUIZ BOOK

ALSO BY JAY ROBERT NASH

Fiction
On All Fronts
A Crime Story

Nonfiction
Dillinger: Dead or Alive?
Citizen Hoover, A Critical Study of the Life and Times
    of J. Edgar Hoover and His F.B.I.
Bloodletters and Badmen, A Narrative Encyclopedia of American
    Criminals from the Pilgrims to the Present
Hustlers and Con Men, An Anecdotal History of the
    Confidence Man and His Games
Darkest Hours, A Narrative Encyclopedia of Worldwide Disasters
    from Ancient Times to the Present
Among the Missing, An Anecdotal History of Missing Persons
    from 1800 to the Present
Murder, America, Homicide in the United States from the
    Revolution to the Present
Almanac of World Crime
People to See: An Anecdotal History of Chicago's
    Makers and Breakers

Poetry
Lost Natives & Expatriates

Theater
The Way Back
Outside the Gates
1947 (Last Rites for the Boys)

THE

TRUE CRIME

QUIZ BOOK

JAY ROBERT NASH

M. EVANS AND COMPANY, INC.
New York

ISBN 0-87131-364-2   CLOTHBOUND

ISBN 0-87131-352-9   PAPERBOUND

M. Evans and Company, Inc.
216 East 49 Street
New York, New York 10017

Design by RFS Graphic Design, Inc.

Manufactured in the United States of America

9 8 7 6 5 4 3 2 1

This book is for Peppy

CONTENTS

The Real McCoy 11
Assassins 15
Con Artists 29
Gangs and Gangsters 41
The Kidnappers 57
The Killers 69
The Lawmen 91
Mouthpieces 105
The Outlaws 117
Prisons and Prisoners 131
The Syndicate 145
Women in Crime 159
Solutions 173

THE
TRUE CRIME
QUIZ BOOK

THE

REAL McCOY

THE

REAL McCOY

The legions of readers devoted to true crime stories are the possessors of encyclopedic minds that catalog the world of real crime and criminals. The fascination here is multilevel, dealing with miscreants of all stripe throughout history, from the kidnapper to the killer, from the blackmailer to the burglar. It is not the fictional Sam Spade's "stuff of dreams," but the hard facts of a world peopled by the Willie Suttons, Al Capones, and Black Barts. It was best summed up by the boxer Kid Mc-Coy, who was sent to San Quentin for the murder of his sweetheart in Los Angeles. A taciturn prisoner, McCoy once blurted to the warden, "You know who I am, don't you—I'm McCoy, not one of those Hollywood types or the kind you find in made-up stories in the pulps. I'm the real McCoy!"

And knowing just who the real McCoys are has become an American pastime, with readers as absorbed by the antics and activities of true-life criminals as others are obsessed by the lives of their fictional counterparts.

Here then is a quiz book for the armchair researchers of factual crime who pride themselves on their special knowledge of the real McCoys, some of whom, no doubt, can give the author, despite years and years of work in these whispering archives, a real run for his money. Certain readers—say, law-enforcement officers—will do well with "Gangs and Gangsters" and "The Syndicate," while secretaries and female violinists will undoubtedly snare most of the answers dealing with "Women and Crime." The author does not expect the professional criminologist to do well, because this book is designed chiefly for the layman, rather than providing "hard data" tests.

Those averaging 50 percent correct answers per quiz should consider themselves well informed about the world of true-fact crime. Anyone scoring 75 percent is a highly perceptive self-styled crime historian. Those who answer 90 percent of the quizzes correctly (with absolutely no cheating, mind you) should be working with the author.

Good luck and happy hunting.

How to Reach a Verdict

No quiz book is complete without a way to check your know-how. There are two ways to score your answers in *The True Crime Quiz Book*. Each chapter is made up of a group of quizzes, A through D, with the more difficult quizzes given a higher point score. As you finish each chapter, you can rate your expertise by checking the solutions (starting on page 173) and totaling your point score to see just how well you know each area of expertise in the true-crime world. At the end of the book, total your points from all the chapters and rate yourself against the masters.

ASSASSINS

ASSASSINS

The assassin, invariably a political creature of warped ambitions, is a particularly odious and spectacular type of killer who strikes down the powerful and the innocent. His actions, unlike those of the professional killer or the mob hit man, are wholly unpredictable, which makes his crime all the more sensational, his reasons inexplicable. Through history, the assassin, representing the unknown, has proved to be the most feared of killers. Following an assassination or an assassination attempt, the killer becomes a cause célèbre, his infamy, oddly enough, becoming equal to his victim's fame, his name forever linked with that of the victim.

The following quizzes test your recall of the world's most sensational assassinations.

QUIZ A

Score 5 points for each correct answer.

1. Match the American assassin with his famous victim.

_____	**1.** Joseph Zangara	**A.** Abraham Lincoln
_____	**2.** Lee Harvey Oswald	**B.** Mayor Anton Cermak
_____	**3.** Julius Guiteau	
_____	**4.** John Wilkes Booth	**C.** William McKinley
_____	**5.** Leon Czolgosz	**D.** James A. Garfield
		E. John F. Kennedy

2. Match the European assassin with his or her famous victim.

_____	**1.** François Ravaillac	**A.** Archduke Francis Ferdinand
_____	**2.** Charlotte Corday	
_____	**3.** Otto Planetta	**B.** Sadi Carnot
_____	**4.** Gavrilo Princip	**C.** Jean Paul Marat
_____	**5.** Santo Caserio	**D.** Henry of Navarre
		E. Engelbert Dollfuss

3. Match the assassin with his native country.

_____	**1.** Prince Felix Yusupov, killer of Rasputin	**A.** Belgium
		B. Russia
_____	**2.** Dr. Carl Austin Weiss, killer of Huey Long	**C.** India
		D. Saudi Arabia
		E. United States

_____ 3. Jacques Mornard,
          killer of Leon
          Trotsky

_____ 4. Nathuram Godse,
          killer of Mahatma
          Gandhi

_____ 5. Musaed Bin
          Abdulaziz, killer of
          King Faisal

4. Match the assassin with the words he uttered when killing his victim.

_____ 1. John Wilkes Booth, **A.** "I done my duty!"
          killer of President
          Lincoln   **B.** "We must now
                                       shoot you."

_____ 2. Leon Czolgosz,
          killer of President   **C.** *Sic semper
          McKinley   tyrannis!* ("Ever
                                       thus to tyrants!")

_____ 3. Jacob Yurovsky,
          killer of Czar   **D.** "If we spare his life,
          Nicholas II of   before the setting
          Russia   of tomorrow's sun
                                       we shall be his
_____ 4. Anonymous bomb   victims."
          thrower, killer of
          Czar Alexander II   **E.** "It's too early to
          of Russia   thank God!"

_____ 5. One of the nine
          assassins who slew
          Czar Paul of Russia

5. Match the victims of assassins with their last words.

_____ **1.** Nicholas II of Russia

_____ **2.** Mahatma Gandhi

_____ **3.** William of Orange

_____ **4.** Julius Caesar

_____ **5.** Caligula

A. "I am still alive!"

B. *"Et tu, Brute?"* ("And you, Brutus?")

C. *"Hai Rama! Hai Rama!"* ("Oh, God! Oh, God!")

D. "My God, have pity on these poor people."

E. "What?"

6. Match the assassin with the motion picture dealing with his killing.

_____ **1.** Aleksei Orlov

_____ **2.** John Wilkes Booth

_____ **3.** Felix Yusupov

_____ **4.** Nathuram Godse

_____ **5.** Jacob Yurovsky

_____ **6.** Dr. Carl Austin Weiss

A. *Nicholas and Alexandra*

B. *Rasputin and the Empress*

C. *Nine Hours to Rama*

D. *The Scarlet Empress*

E. *All the King's Men*

F. *Prince of Players*

QUIZ B

The following statements are either true or false. Score 3 points for each correct answer.

1. John Wilkes Booth, an actor, was prompted to assassinate President Abraham Lincoln because of a bad review.   True or False?

2. Leon Czolgosz was inspired to assassinate President William McKinley after reading about the killing of King Humbert I of Italy by Gaetano Bresci. True or False?

3. The simpleminded Czar Peter III was assassinated at the instigation of his wife, Catherine.   True or False?

4. Roman Emperor Claudius was assassinated at the instigation of his wife Messalina.   True or False?

5. Thomas à Becket, the Archbishop of Canterbury, was assassinated because of his religious convictions.   True or False?

6. Alexander the Great rose to power in Macedonia through his mother, Olympias, who planned the assassination of his father, Philip.   True or False?

7. Lee Harvey Oswald was assassinated by Jack Ruby on November 23, 1964.   True or False?

8. Sirhan Sirhan, who assassinated Senator Robert F. Kennedy, was a member of the Irish Republican Army.   True or False?

9. President James A. Garfield lingered for two months before dying of an assassin's bullet in 1881.   True or False?

10. Rafael Trujillo, dictator of the Dominican Republic, shot it out with his assassins before being fatally wounded in a 1961 ambush.   True or False?

11. President Park Chung Hee of South Korea was assassinated in 1979 on orders of the country's CIA chief, Kim Jae Kyu.   True or False?

12. The assassination of Emperor Claudius took place on the Ides of March.   True or False?

13. The Roman Emperor Caligula was assassinated by members of his own palace guard.   True or False?

14. James Earl Ray confessed to the assassination of Martin Luther King Jr.   True or False?

15. Adolf Hitler secretly planned the assassination of Engelbert Dollfuss of Austria.   True or False?

QUIZ C

Down through history, most famous victims of assassination were taken unawares by their assailants. What were the following victims doing when assassinated? Score 4 points for each correct answer.

1. President John F. Kennedy was

   _____ **A.** getting out of an airplane.

   _____ **B.** riding in a motorcade.

   _____ **C.** sitting down to dinner.

2. President James A. Garfield was

_____ **A.** strolling in a Washington, D.C., park.

_____ **B.** having a haircut.

_____ **C.** entering a train station.

3. President Abraham Lincoln was

_____ **A.** upbraiding a servant in the White House.

_____ **B.** reading the New York *Times.*

_____ **C.** watching a play.

4. Jean Paul Marat was

_____ **A.** taking a bath.

_____ **B.** sketching a nude.

_____ **C.** having a tooth extracted.

5. Senator Robert F. Kennedy had just

_____ **A.** bought a hot dog.

_____ **B.** finished a speech.

_____ **C.** called his brother.

6. Martin Luther King, Jr., was

_____ **A.** writing a report.

_____ **B.** leading a march.

_____ **C.** standing on a balcony.

7. Ngo Dinh Diem was

_____ **A.** riding in an armored personnel carrier.

_____ **B.** inspecting his palace shock troops.

_____ **C.** sipping champagne at a reception.

8. Leon Trotsky was

_____ **A.** seated at his desk, writing.

_____ **B.** arguing with his wife.

_____ **C.** delivering a harangue to Mexican peasants.

9. Reinhard Heydrich, the SS leader in Czechoslovakia, was

_____ **A.** torturing prisoners.

_____ **B.** watching atrocity films.

_____ **C.** riding in his car.

10. Julius Caesar was

_____ **A.** entering the Roman Senate building.

_____ **B.** dallying with Cleopatra.

_____ **C.** consulting the Oracle of Delphi.

QUIZ D

Use your deductive reasoning, the process of elimination, and your instincts to match the assassin with his personality and historical profile. Score 5 points for each correct answer.

1. John Wilkes Booth
2. Nathuram Godse
3. Dr. Carl Austin Weiss
4. Joseph Zangara
5. Sirhan Sirhan

6. Lee Harvey Oswald
7. James Earl Ray
8. Felix Yusupov
9. Julius Guiteau
10. Leon Czolgosz

_____ A. A political malcontent, he went to Russia to study communism and returned to the United States to join the "Fair Play for Cuba" movement.

_____ B. Mentally disturbed and physically ill, this dwarfish assassin moved to Miami, Florida, to be on hand when President-elect Roosevelt visited that city in 1933.

_____ C. A Southern sympathizer throughout the Civil War, who took his bows and kudos in the heart of the Union, he was a megalomaniac who thought of himself as an avenging angel.

_____ **D.** He was a prince who thought to serve the crown by assassinating a monster. Later he lived in European exile, and he died in New York in 1967, a practitioner of faith healing to the end.

_____ **E.** A young zealot, he struck down a much-beloved man to "purify" his religion, maintaining to the moment of his execution that he had rendered his land a great service.

_____ **F.** Unbalanced, he stalked the President for weeks, planning his assassination, his revenge for not receiving a political appointment he thought due him. He defended himself at his trial, cursing the judge, prosecuting attorney, and jury. He recited a poem of his own composition before being hanged.

_____ **G.** A sensitive and compassionate young man; his motives for assassinating a political despot involved family honor.

_____ **H.** This impoverished, rather cretinous anarchist traveled to Buffalo, New York, to assassinate the President, who was attending the Pan-American Exposition. He reached out as if to shake the President's hand, his revolver covered by a handkerchief, and fired.

_____ **I.** A youthful zealot; his motives for slaying his famous victim have never been revealed to this day. He confessed to the assassination and is in jail in California.

_____ **J.** He had a long criminal and prison record
before shooting down the greatest Civil
Rights leader of the day. He later escaped
prison but was recaptured and remains in
prison at this writing.

SCORING

Quiz A   _____

Quiz B   _____

Quiz C   _____

Quiz D   _____

   Chapter Total Score   _____

Your Bodyguard Rating

If you scored   You should apply to the Secret Ser-
between 315 and 290   vice immediately.

If you scored   You'd know who the dangerous per-
between 289 and 152   son was in a crowd.

If you scored   Don't attend any ceremonies where
between 151 and 0   public figures are present.

CON

ARTISTS

CON

ARTISTS

The swindler or con artist is considered, by virtue of his high intelligence and witty schemes, to be today's dean of criminals. In the past, the con artist proved himself (or herself) to be the most inventive and elusive of felons, and since the motion picture *The Sting*, this breed of criminal has captured the public's imagination, particularly since he preys upon victims whose greed invites financial ruination.

Here then, in the following quizzes, is a challenge to the reader to recall those spectacular sharpers whose scams and flimflams made criminal history.

QUIZ A

Score 4 points for each correct answer.

1. Match the con artist with his sobriquet.

_____ **1.** Joseph Weil   **A.** "The Postal Kid"

_____ **2.** Victor Lustig   **B.** "Soapy"

_____ **3.** Jefferson Randolph   **C.** "The Count"
Smith
                        D. "The Yellow Kid"

_____ **4.** Alvin Clarence   **E.** "Titanic"
Thompson

_____ **5.** James W. Ryan

2. Match the con artist with his special scam.

_____ **1.** Canada Bill Jones   **A.** The magic wallet

_____ **2.** Reed Waddell   **B.** Three-card monte

_____ **3.** William Elmer Mead   **C.** Salting diamond
mines
_____ **4.** Fred "Deacon"
Buckminster   **D.** The gold brick

_____ **5.** Philip Arnold and   **E.** The pedigree dog
John Slack

3. Match the con artist with the city in which he operated.

_____ **1.** The Gondorf   **A.** Washington, D.C.
Brothers
                        B. New York

_____ **2.** Joseph Weil
                        C. Boston

_____ **3.** Lou Blonger
                        D. Denver

_____ **4.** Charlie Ponzi
                        E. Chicago

_____ **5.** Gaston B. Means

4. Match the con artist with his native land.

_____	**1.** Serge Rubinstein	**A.**	United States
_____	**2.** Ivar Kreuger	**B.**	France
_____	**3.** Alves Reis	**C.**	Sweden
_____	**4.** Donald Coster	**D.**	Russia
_____	**5.** Serge Stavisky	**E.**	Portugal

5. Match the con artist with his famous victim.

_____	**1.** Victor Lustig	**A.**	Henry Astor
_____	**2.** "Lord Gordon-Gordon"	**B.**	Oscar Wilde
		C.	Al Capone
_____	**3.** "Hungry Joe" Lewis	**D.**	Evalyn Walsh McLean
_____	**4.** Gaston B. Means		
_____	**5.** Daniel Drew	**E.**	Jay Gould

QUIZ B

The following statements are either true or false. Score 3 points for each correct answer.

1. In con parlance, a "sucker" means a victim. True or False?

2. The Poillon Sisters of New York were notorious female sharpers who practiced the matrimonial con. True or False?

3. The enormous scams practiced by Serge Stavisky brought down a French government. True or False?

4. Con man "Big Jim" Fisk bilked President Grant out of $100,000.   True or False?

5. A "money box" is a con game employing a box which purportedly makes money.   True or False?

6. The "inside man" is the confederate who inveigles a victim into a con game.   True or False?

7. "Big Mike" McDonald was king of the con men in Chicago for a decade, even controlling the city government and the mayor.   True or False?

8. Wilson Mizener scammed Al Jolson by renting him the Winter Garden Theater in New York with a fake lease.   True or False?

9. Con man Gaston B. Means had once been a member of the Bureau of Investigation in Washington, D.C. True or False?

10. Comedian Jack Benny lost $300,000 in the massive Home Stake Production Company oil swindle in 1974. True or False?

QUIZ C

Score 4 points for each correct identification.

1. He sold the Eiffel Tower twice to duped investors.
   _____ **A.** Adolph "Kid" Duff
   _____ **B.** Victor Lustig
   _____ **C.** George "Hump" McManus

2. He formed a Boston bank, paying enormous interest to depositors in a multimillion-dollar Peter-to-Paul scheme.

_____ **A.** John Dillinger

_____ **B.** Charles Ponzi

_____ **C.** "Red Jimmy" Fitzgerald

3. He rented vacant Midwestern banks, peopled them with phony customers, and pretended to be the bank president as a front for his colossal swindles.

_____ **A.** Joseph Weil

_____ **B.** Charles Arthur "Pretty Boy" Floyd

_____ **C.** George "The Kentucky Gentlemen" Mitchell

4. He pretended to be a lost and down-and-out friend of recently deceased persons in order to receive cash gifts from the bereaved family.

_____ **A.** The "Hashhouse Kid"

_____ **B.** "Sorrowful" Jones

_____ **C.** Thomas "Mournful" Meeker

5. He married dozens of women in matrimonial swindles for decades, becoming the "Bluebeard of con."

_____ **A.** Jackie French

_____ **B.** Sigmund Engle

_____ **C.** "Gas" Grosch

6. They were masters of the "Big Store" at the turn of the century.

_____ **A.** The Gondorf Brothers

_____ **B.** The Poillon Sisters

_____ **C.** The Dalton Brothers

7. Con artists supreme, they owned and operated the town of Denver during the early 1920s.

_____ **A.** Joseph Weil and Fred Buckminster

_____ **B.** Lou Blonger and Adolph "Kid" Duff

_____ **C.** Melvin Purvis and Harry Anslinger

8. He watered his livestock (one of the first business cons in America) and became a millionaire.

_____ **A.** Jay Gould

_____ **B.** "Big Jim" Fisk

_____ **C.** Daniel Drew

9. He invented the fantastic "Mississippi Bubble" scam in 1717.

_____ **A.** "Lord Gordon-Gordon"

_____ **B.** John Law

_____ **C.** Robert Harley

10. He not only sold the Galata Bridge, which spans the Golden Horn, he convinced a sucker to pay him for the _Orient Express_.

_____ **A.** Donald Coster

_____ **B.** Joseph Weil

_____ **C.** Sülün Osman

QUIZ D

Match the con artists with the following profiles. Score 5 points for each correct answer.

1. Joseph Weil
2. Fred "Deacon" Buckminster
3. Victor Lustig
4. William Elmer Mead
5. Jefferson Randolph Smith
6. The Williamson Clan
7. The Burr Brothers

8. Ivar Kreuger
9. Charles Ponzi
10. Donald Coster
11. Abram Sykowski
12. Serge Stavisky
13. Leo Koretz
14. James Addison Reavis
15. Marcus Garvey

_____ **A.** He forged Spanish land grants which purportedly left his ancestors almost all of the state of Arizona, then demanded that the railroads and mining interests in the state pay him exorbitant fees for using "his" land. He was dubbed "The Baron of Arizona."

_____ **B.** A con man all his life, he worked in the Midwest with a famous partner, and wound up teaching mathematics in Michigan State Prison.

_____ **C.** He was a master of three-card monte, the gold brick, and all the other ancient con games. Migrating to Alaska, he virtually controlled all activities in Skagway for a decade.

_____ **D.** He lived to be 101 and was considered to be the dean of American con men, a man who dressed in sartorial splendor and was addicted to reading a turn-of-the-century comic strip, "Hogan's Alley."

_____ **E.** This Chicago hustler sold phony South American oil stock to Midwest tycoons. A diabetic, after his exposure he committed suicide by gobbling down an enormous box of chocolates.

_____ **F.** This black con artist mulcted his own people in a wild scheme whereby he promised to take all American Negroes back to Africa to found a new nation.

_____ **G.** His real name was Philip Musica and, under an alias, he bilked some of the largest drug firms in the country, draining away their stock. He committed suicide in the bathroom of his mansion as police arrived to arrest him.

_____ **H.** They are drifters who roam the country, scamming for small amounts, victimizing average citizens. Most of their cons involve house repairs which are never really performed.

_____ **I.** He was a "Big Store" operator who established fake banks and manipulated stocks. After a long prison term, he traveled to Italy, where he audaciously bilked Mussolini before going to South America to retire.

_____ **J.** A suave international con man, he pretended to have millions in banks, fortunes that could be released only after he paid enormous legal fees, these fees being scammed from his wealthy victims, King Farouk included.

_____ **K.** J. Edgar Hoover called this master con man "the meanest man on earth." He once leased ball parks so crowds could witness "the end of the world."

_____ **L.** He was known as the "Match King," and he borrowed millions against stocks he had forged. He committed suicide in Paris.

_____ **M.** He conned his way through Europe before coming to the United States, where he was finally arrested by federal agents, although he managed a spectacular escape from the FBI's detention center in Washington, D.C., in 1935 before being sent to Leavenworth.

_____ **N.** They specialized in phony mining stock with tip-off names—Rawhide Tarantula, Montezuma Mining and Smelting, and Golden Fleece Mining.

_____ **O.** He committed suicide, officials later reported, after his scam was unearthed, although some claim today that he was murdered to cover up his high-level contacts. A major film was based on his life.

SCORING

Quiz A   _____

Quiz B   _____

Quiz C   _____

Quiz D   _____

   Chapter Total Score   _____

Your Bunco Squad Rating

If you scored between 245 and 196

You're sharper than the best "Big Store" operators.

If you scored between 195 and 66

No "short con" escapes your notice.

If you scored between 65 and 0

If a stranger points out a fat wallet on the sidewalk, keep moving.

GANGS

AND

GANGSTERS

GANGS

AND

GANGSTERS

The gang and its members have been with the U.S. since the early 1800s, beginning in the growing cities of the East and spreading west with the pioneers, mushrooming in each new city to grab off whatever illegitimate enterprises were available or could be created. The gangster, though emulated in Europe and particularly in today's Japan, has always been identified as a homegrown American breed, which during the 1920s and 1930s took on an almost heroic image, replacing the concept of the pioneer.

Nurtured undoubtedly by his own sense of power and place, the gangster fostered the self-image of being a local folk hero, someone for street youths to follow. In the "yellow" days of the press, the gangster, indeed, became an offbeat celebrity, much to the delight of the Al Capones and Dutch Schultzes. He is now anonymously hidden beneath the umbrella of the syndicate, but during his public heyday Mr. Gangster boldly strutted American streets, his suit coat bulging with a revolver, creating his own terrible history and reveling in it. The learned reader of such nostalgia will certainly do well with the following quizzes.

QUIZ A

Score 5 points for each correct answer.

1. Match the gang with its native city.

_____ **1.** Five Points Gang   **A.** Denver

_____ **2.** 42 Gang   **B.** St. Louis

_____ **3.** Lou Blonger Gang   **C.** Detroit

_____ **4.** Eagan's Rats   **D.** Chicago

_____ **5.** Purple Mob   **E.** New York

2. Match the gangster with his first gang.

_____ **1.** Al Capone   **A.** Little Augie Orgen
                                          Gang
_____ **2.** Sam Giancana
                                     B. Five Points Gang
_____ **3.** Jack Diamond
                                     C. 42 Gang
_____ **4.** Abe "Kid Twist"
         Reles   **D.** Al Capone Gang

_____ **5.** Tony Accardo   **E.** Bug & Meyer Gang

3. Match the gangster with the gang leader who sponsored his career.

_____ **1.** Al Capone   **A.** Arnold Rothstein

_____ **2.** Jack Diamond   **B.** "Big Jim" Colosimo

_____ **3.** Willie Moretti   **C.** Johnny Torrio

_____ **4.** Vincent Coll   **D.** Frank Costello

_____ **5.** Johnny Torrio   **E.** Dutch Schultz

4. Match the gang with the era of its prominence.

_____ **1.** Al Capone Gang   **A.** 1900s

_____ **2.** Monk Eastman Gang   **B.** 1910s

         C. 1920s

_____ **3.** Dopey Benny Gang   **D.** 1930s

_____ **4.** 42 Gang   **E.** 1940s

_____ **5.** Duchess Spinelli Gang

5. Match the gangster with his crime specialty.

_____ **1.** Al Capone   **A.** Prostitution

_____ **2.** "Lucky" Luciano   **B.** Labor racketeering

_____ **3.** Lepke Buchalter   **C.** Bootlegging

_____ **4.** Larry Fay   **D.** Narcotics

_____ **5.** Albert Anastasia   **E.** Milk racketeering

6. Match the gangster with his ethnic origin.

_____ **1.** Meyer Lansky   **A.** Irish

_____ **2.** Al Capone   **B.** Russian

_____ **3.** "Lucky" Luciano   **C.** Italian

_____ **4.** Dion O'Bannion   **D.** Polish

_____ **5.** Earl Weiss   **E.** Sicilian

7. Match the gangster with his atrocity and/or gangland killing.

_____ **1.** Al Capone	**A.** The killing of Dion O'Bannion
_____ **2.** Frankie Yale	
_____ **3.** Verne Miller	**B.** The St. Valentine's Day Massacre
_____ **4.** Carlo Gambino	**C.** The killing of "Dutch" Schultz
_____ **5.** Charles "The Bug" Workman	**D.** The Kansas City Massacre
	E. The killing of Albert Anastasia

8. Match the gangsters with their favorite pastimes.

_____ **1.** Al Capone	**A.** Broadway musicals
_____ **2.** Samuel J. "Nails" Morton	**B.** Dancing at parties
	C. Horse riding
_____ **3.** Dion O'Bannion	**D.** Tending flowers
_____ **4.** "Lucky" Luciano	**E.** Baseball games
_____ **5.** Waxey Gordon	

9. Match the gangster with his partner who was either kidnapped or shot by rival gangsters.

_____ **1.** Owney Madden	**A.** "Big Frenchy" DeMange
_____ **2.** Roger "The Terrible" Touhy	**B.** Johnny Torrio
	C. Matt Kolb
_____ **3.** Al Capone	**D.** "Lucky" Luciano
_____ **4.** George Moran	**E.** Dion O'Bannion
_____ **5.** Benjamin Siegel	

10. Match the gangster with what he was doing when he was killed.

_____ **1.** Joe "The Boss" Masseria

_____ **2.** Jack Diamond

_____ **3.** Dutch Schultz

_____ **4.** Vincent Coll

_____ **5.** Jack Zuta

A. Sleeping off a drunk

B. Eating spaghetti

C. Putting nickels into a jukebox

D. Going to the washroom

E. Making an extortion call in a phone booth

11. Match the gangster with the motion picture star who enacted his life.

_____ **1.** John Dillinger

_____ **2.** "Baby Face" Nelson

_____ **3.** Jack Diamond

_____ **4.** Arnold Rothstein

_____ **5.** Roger Touhy

_____ **6.** Clyde Barrow

_____ **7.** Al Capone

A. Preston Foster

B. Rod Steiger

C. Warren Beatty

D. Lawrence Tierney

E. Mickey Rooney

F. David Janssen

G. Ray Danton

12. Match the gangster with the motion picture dealing with his life.

_____ **1.** Francis "Two-Gun" Crowley

_____ **2.** Al Capone

_____ **3.** "Terrible Tommy" O'Connor

_____ **4.** John Dillinger

_____ **5.** Dion O'Bannion

_____ **6.** Arnold Rothstein

_____ **7.** Herman "Beansie" Rosenthal

A. _Underworld_

B. _Angels with Dirty Faces_

C. _Musketeers of Pig Alley_

D. _Unholy Alliance_

E. _Little Caesar_

F. _The Petrified Forest_

G. _Public Enemy_

13. Match the gangster with his sobriquet.

_____ **1.** Vincent Coll

_____ **2.** Al Capone

_____ **3.** Charles Luciano

_____ **4.** George Moran

_____ **5.** Benjamin Siegel

_____ **6.** Jack Diamond

_____ **7.** Earl Weiss

_____ **8.** Frank Wortman

_____ **9.** Vincent Drucci

A. "Bugs"

B. "Buster"

C. "Hymie"

D. "Mad Dog"

E. "Scarface"

F. "Lucky"

G. "Legs"

H. "The Schemer"

I. "Bugsy"

14. Match the gangster with his most memorable line.

_____ **1.** Benjamin Siegel

_____ **2.** Al Capone

_____ **3.** Monk Eastman

_____ **4.** George Moran

_____ **5.** Dion O'Bannion

A. "To hell with them Sicilians!"

B. "You gotta knock your man out!"

C. "I will live and let live."

D. "We only kill each other."

E. "Only Capone kills like that."

15. Match the sobriquet with the gangster's last name.

_____ **1.** "Big Mike"

_____ **2.** "Big Jim"

_____ **3.** "Big Jack"

_____ **4.** "Big Tim"

_____ **5.** "Big Josh"

_____ **6.** "Big Bill"

A. Lingley

B. Murphy

C. Hines

D. Colosimo

E. McDonald

F. Zelig

QUIZ B

The following statements are either true or false. Score 3 points for each correct answer.

1. Al Capone's two livid scars were on the right side of his face.   True or False?

2. Jack Diamond was also known as "the clay pigeon" because he had been shot many times.   True or False?

3. Meyer Lansky and Bugsy Siegel began their criminal careers together as teenagers.   True or False?

4. Nathan "Kid Dropper" Kaplan, a New York gangster, took his nickname after an old-time prizefighter named "Jack the Dropper."   True or False?

5. "Diamond Joe" Esposito was Al Capone's first boss in Chicago.   True or False?

6. Jack Dragna was the first crime kingpin of Los Angeles before the arrival of Bugsy Siegel.   True or False?

7. Spike O'Donnell, a fierce leader of a bootleg gang on Chicago's South Side in the early 1920s, told a reporter: "I can lick this bird Capone if he'll just fight with bare knuckles!"   True or False?

8. The Genna Brothers of Chicago were bootleg allies of the Bugs Moran Gang.   True or False?

9. Capone enforcer Sam "Golf Bag" Hunt carried a machine gun in his golf bag.   True or False?

10. Johnny Lazia was the underworld chieftain of Kansas City, Missouri, who carried out the orders of Boss Pendergast.   True or False?

QUIZ C

Score 4 points for each correct answer.

1. Who was known as "The Enforcer" in the Capone gang?

    _____ **A.** Murray "The Camel" Humphreys

    _____ **B.** Charles Fischetti

    _____ **C.** Frank Nitti

2. Which Brooklyn gangster in the 1920s manufactured his own cigars with his picture on the box?

    _____ **A.** Max Zwerbach

    _____ **B.** Frankie Yale

    _____ **C.** Paul Kelly

3. Which Chicago gangster purchased an entire town in northern Wisconsin and forced the residents to name the place after him?

    _____ **A.** "Polack Joe" Saltis

    _____ **B.** Frank "Lefty" Koncil

    _____ **C.** John "Mitters" Foley

4. Which New York gangster was shot six times by eleven hoodlums in 1912 but lived to become one of the ruling bootleggers of the 1920s?

    _____ **A.** Joe Adonis

    _____ **B.** Owney Madden

    _____ **C.** Vito Genovese

5. Who was known in the New York underworld as "The Artichoke King"?

_____ **A.** Vito "Socko" Gurino

_____ **B.** Ciro Terranova

_____ **C.** Angelo Catalano

6. Which Chicago gangster of the early 1920s ordered his henchmen to don top hats and tails and accompany him to the opera?

_____ **A.** William "Klondike" O'Donnell

_____ **B.** Ralph Sheldon

_____ **C.** Dion O'Bannion

7. Who among New York gangsters was known as "Gurrah" after his marble-mouthed delivery of "Get out of here!"?

_____ **A.** Jacob Shapiro

_____ **B.** Chick Tricker

_____ **C.** Jack Sirocco

8. Which murderous duo performed Capone's special killings?

_____ **A.** "Polack Joe" Saltis and Frankie McErlane

_____ **B.** Frankie Lake and Terry Druggan

_____ **C.** John Scalise and Albert Anselmi

9. Special Prosecutor Thomas E. Dewey was ordered to break up New York rackets in 1935. One gang overlord declared: "Dewey's my nemesis—he's gotta go!" Who was he?

_____ **A.** "Dutch" Schultz

_____ **B.** Frank "Chink" Sherman

_____ **C.** Vannie Higgins

10. Bootlegger Samuel J. "Nails" Morton was thrown from his horse in Chicago's Lincoln Park bridle path and kicked to death. His gangster sidekick avenged his death by shooting the horse. Who was this underworld zany?

_____ **A.** John "Dingbat" Oberta

_____ **B.** Louis "Two-Gun" Alterie

_____ **C.** Samuzzo "Samoots" Amatuna

QUIZ D

Match the gangster with his profile. Score 5 points for each correct answer.

1. "Dutch" Schultz
2. Owney Madden
3. Waxey Gordon
4. Al Capone
5. Vincent Coll
6. Jake and Harry Guzik
7. Joe Esposito
8. Frank and Pete Gusenberg
9. Paul Kelly
10. Harry Horowitz

_____ **A.** He was known as "Gyp the Blood" and was one of New York's most cold-blooded gunmen of the 1910s, one of the four gangsters who shot down Herman "Beansie" Rosenthal on the orders of crooked cop Charles Becker. He went to the electric chair wearing a sneer.

_____ **B.** He was called "The Killer" and had been a star member of New York's "Gopher Gang"; he rose to prominence during Prohibition and was one of the few big-time bootleggers to retire unmolested (in Hot Springs, Arkansas).

_____ **C.** They were panderers, these brothers who worked for Capone, one of whom had the nickname "Greasy Thumb" because he was once a waiter and his thumb kept slipping into the soup bowls he carried.

_____ **D.** He began as a bouncer in Johnny Torrio's Four Deuces Café in Chicago in 1920. Four years later he literally ran the city.

_____ **E.** He started in the New York rackets as a gunsel for "Dutch" Schultz, then became his employer's rival, a wild killer who once shot a child while gunning for the Dutchman's men.

_____ **F.** These brothers worked for "Bugs" Moran and were the two top gunmen of Moran's mob killed in the St. Valentine's Day Massacre.

_____ **G.** His real name was Irving Wexler, and when he wasn't running bootleg hooch, he was attending Broadway musicals, some of which he financed.

_____ **H.** Addicted to wearing diamond cuff links, stickpin, and rings, he was first a Capone ally, then a Capone victim, shot down in view of his wife.

_____ **I.** He shared the boss rule of New York with Kid Spanish and Nathan Kaplan in the 1900s; he was the leader of the Five Points Gang.

_____ **J.** His real name was Arthur Flegenheimer and he was one of the bootleg barons of New York during the 1920s; he was shot to death on orders of the newly formed syndicate in 1935. As he lay dying, half conscious in a hospital, he uttered the cryptic words: "A boy has never wept nor dashed a thousand kim."

SCORING

Quiz A   _____

Quiz B   _____

Quiz C   _____

Quiz D   _____

    Chapter Total Score   _____

Your "G-Man" Rating

If you scored between 540 and 396

The FBI has desperate need of your services.

If you scored between 395 and 136

You should be running a rogue's gallery.

If you scored between 135 and 0

Don't bring up the name of Melvin Purvis.

THE

KIDNAPPERS

THE

KIDNAPPERS

No other crime arouses such passion along a broad public base as does kidnapping. Until this century, kidnapping was a rare occurrence around the world. The first significant American kidnapping took place in 1874, but the crime did not reach epidemic proportions until the gangsters of the 1930s realized that enormous profits, far in excess of what banks had to offer, could be reaped by kidnapping the wealthy.

With the rash of kidnappings at that time, tough federal laws were enacted making the crime a capital offense and allowing the FBI and other federal agencies to pursue kidnappers across any state line, as they did bank robbers.

Still, kidnappers flourished through the decades. In the 1970s kidnapping became a method by which political terrorists pressed their demands.

The quizzes that follow will challenge the memories of those who first read of sensational kidnappings in shocking headlines, as well as heard similar grim announcements on TV.

QUIZ A

Score 5 points for each correct answer.

1. Match the kidnap victim with the kidnapper.

_____ 1. Bobbie Greenlease, Jr.

_____ 2. Charles F. Urschel

_____ 3. Edward G. Bremer

_____ 4. Suzanne Degnan

_____ 5. Bobbie Franks

_____ 6. Charles Lindbergh, Jr.

A. The Barker Gang

B. Bruno Richard Hauptmann

C. Bonnie Heady and Carl Austin Hall

D. Nathan Leopold and Richard Loeb

E. William Heirens

F. The Machine Gun Kelly Gang

2. Match the kidnap victim with the state in which the crime took place.

_____ 1. Weyerhaeuser

_____ 2. Lindbergh

_____ 3. Greenlease

_____ 4. Degnan

_____ 5. Bremer

A. Illinois

B. Washington

C. Missouri

D. Minnesota

E. New Jersey

3. Match the foreign diplomat with the country in which he was kidnapped.

_____ **1.** James R. Cross   **A.** Brazil

_____ **2.** Eugene Beihl   **B.** Guatemala

_____ **3.** Daniel A. Mitrone   **C.** Uruguay

_____ **4.** Sean M. Holly   **D.** Canada

_____ **5.** Giovanni E. Bucher   **E.** Spain

4. Match the kidnap victim with those thought to be responsible for the kidnapping.

_____ **1.** Aldo Moro   **A.** The Mafia

_____ **2.** James Hoffa   **B.** The SLA

_____ **3.** Patricia Hearst   **C.** The syndicate

_____ **4.** J. Paul Getty III   **D.** The Red Brigades

_____ **5.** Eugene Beihl   **E.** Basque separatists

5. Match the kidnap victim with the amount demanded for his or her release.

_____ **1.** William A. Hamm, Jr.   **A.** $100,000

       B. $200,000

_____ **2.** Charles F. Urschel   **C.** $250,000

_____ **3.** Bobbie Greenlease, Jr.   **D.** $500,000

       E. $600,000

_____ **4.** Kenneth King

_____ **5.** Barbara Jane Mackle

QUIZ B

The following statements are either true or false. Score 3 points for each correct answer.

1. The largest ransom in modern kidnapping history, $2.9 million, was paid for the release of J. Paul Getty III in 1973.   True or False?

2. Charles Brewster Ross was the first kidnap victim in American history.   True or False?

3. Henry VIII of England was kidnapped and held in the Tower of London for a huge ransom.   True or False?

4. Richard the Lion-Hearted of England was held in Austria for a $15 million ransom by Emperor Henry VI.   True or False?

5. Pat Crowe, the kidnapper of Edward A. Cudahy, Jr., actually paid back the ransom he received after reforming years later.   True or False?

6. Willa Whitla, kidnapped in 1909, was murdered by his kidnappers.   True or False?

7. Marian Parker, kidnapped by William E. Hickman in 1927, was returned safely to her home.   True or False?

8. Alice Speed Stoll was kidnapped by Thomas Robinson, Jr., in 1934.   True or False?

9. Generalissimo Chiang Kai-shek was kidnapped in 1936 by a warlord under his command.   True or False?

10. Bonnie Heady and her lover Carl Austin Hall went to the gas chamber for kidnapping Bobbie Greenlease, Jr.   True or False?

QUIZ C

Score 4 points for each correct answer.

1. What evidence was discovered that helped to lead to the arrest and conviction of Bruno Richard Hauptmann as the kidnapper of the Lindbergh baby?

   _____ **A.** A nightshirt

   _____ **B.** Part of the ransom money

   _____ **C.** A spare tire

2. Hauptmann, a carpenter with a long criminal record, left a telltale piece of evidence at the scene of the kidnapping. What was it?

   _____ **A.** A hammer with his fingerprints on it

   _____ **B.** Two chisels with his initials on the handles

   _____ **C.** A ladder made from the boards of his attic

3. William Hamm, Jr., kidnapped by the Barker Gang in 1933, was a wealthy

   _____ **A.** locksmith.

   _____ **B.** brewer.

   _____ **C.** banker.

4. To prove to J. Paul Getty, the world's richest man, that his grandson was indeed being held for ransom, the kidnappers

_____ **A.** cut off the boy's ear and mailed it to a newspaper.

_____ **B.** sent the youth's fingerprints on a post-card to Scotland Yard.

_____ **C.** took photos of the grandson while he was sleeping and sent these to authorities.

5. Another man helped "Machine Gun" Kelly kidnap Oklahoma oil man Charles Urschel. Who was he?

_____ **A.** Harvey Bailey

_____ **B.** Albert Bates

_____ **C.** Wilbur Underhill

6. Edward J. Cudahy, Jr., kidnapped by Pat Crowe in 1900, came from a wealthy

_____ **A.** steel family.

_____ **B.** railroad family.

_____ **C.** meat-packing family.

7. It was reported that President Theodore Roosevelt was ready to go to war with Morocco over the kidnapping of a rich American by a local chief named Rassouli. What was the victim's name?

_____ **A.** Ion Perdicaris

_____ **B.** Elmer Hoxie

_____ **C.** K. L. Palmer

8. Richard Loeb, who kidnapped and killed Bobbie Franks in 1924, thought to commit the perfect crime. So bold was Loeb that he actually

_____ **A.** attempted to help investigators with the case.

_____ **B.** made midnight phone calls in which he challenged police to catch him.

_____ **C.** burned his initials on the clothing of the Franks child.

9. Loeb's partner, Nathan Leopold, left a telltale piece of evidence at the murder site. What was it?

_____ **A.** His fraternity ring

_____ **B.** The typewriter on which he had typed the ransom note

_____ **C.** His glasses

10. Thomas Harold Thurmond and John Maurice Holmes, the kidnappers of Brooke Hart, were dragged from their jail cells in San Jose, California, on November 26, 1933, by a mob of more than fifteen thousand and hanged. What motion picture is based on this incident?

_____ **A.** *Black Fury*

_____ **B.** *Fury*

_____ **C.** *Fury at Furnace Creek*

QUIZ D

Match the kidnapper with the profile of his life. Score 5 points for each correct answer.

1. Loeb and Leopold

2. Gary Steven Krist

3. Donald DeFreeze

4. Albert Fish

5. John Henry Seadlund

6. Thurmond and Holmes

7. William Heirens

8. George "Machine Gun" Kelly

9. William Westervelt

10. William Moster and Joseph Douglass

_____ A. They were two impoverished youths who originally thought to kidnap a wealthy youth to pay a small amount of bills. One of them was apprehended in a phone booth, still arguing over the ransom.

_____ B. He was sent to prison for life, a much over-rated gangster who wrote to his kidnap victim shortly before his death in 1954: "These five words seem written in fire on the walls of my cell: Nothing can be worth this!"

_____ C. He was called "The Moon Maniac" and "The Cannibal," an elderly man who was executed for kidnapping and murdering children.

_____ **D.** He kidnapped wealthy Illinois businessman Charles S. Ross, killed his victim after receiving a $50,000 ransom, and fled to California. He was arrested by FBI agents while placing a bet at the Santa Anita racetrack, and was electrocuted.

_____ **E.** They abducted Charles Brewster Ross and were later caught and shot robbing a home in Brooklyn. They confessed the kidnapping with their dying breaths.

_____ **F.** He masterminded the kidnapping of Charlie Ross and was given a prison term for the crime, but never revealed what happened to the four-year-old boy.

_____ **G.** He was a professional burglar who killed women he found in the apartments he invaded. After one burglary in Chicago in 1946 he allegedly wrote on the wall: "Catch me before I kill more, I can't help myself." He was finally apprehended and sent to prison for life for kidnapping and killing Suzanne Degnan.

_____ **H.** A kidnapper who thought his intellect superior to the law, he held his captive, Barbara Jane Mackle, in an underground tomb while demanding an enormous ransom.

_____ **I.** They believed in the myth of the "Superman," and thought to commit the perfect crime. Their lives were spared through the inventive defense mounted by Clarence Darrow. Two movies, *Rope* and *Compulsion*, were based on their crime.

_____ **J.** He was a political fanatic who reportedly kidnapped Patty Hearst and later died in a wild
gun battle with police.

SCORING

Quiz A   _____

Quiz B   _____

Quiz C   _____

Quiz D   _____

    Chapter Total Score   _____

Your Detective Rating

**If you scored
between 250 and 196**
You'd have the abductors collared
in an hour.

**If you scored
between 195 and 86**
You'd recover the ransom.

**If you scored
between 85 and 0**
Order new locks for your doors and
windows.

THE

KILLERS

THE

KILLERS

Murder takes all forms (and types to perform them), from lonely domestic killing to mass slayings that muddle comprehension and remedy. As the most serious crime, homicide produces a plethora of motivations and, in the light of trial and conviction, the most astounding personalities in the annals of crime.

These personalities have provided literature and motion pictures with gritty grist, unforgettable nightmare figures that are so outlandish, so incredible that it is difficult to believe that these cold-blooded creatures are human at all and not the steaming specters of some mad novelist's explosive imagination.

The Landrus, Haarmanns, and Kurtens who brought terror to Europe are equally matched in America by mass killers H. H. Holmes, Jesse Pomeroy, "Son of Sam," and John Wayne Gacy. In contrast to the human monsters emerging from the shadows of each era are those figures who gleaned as much attention and public awe for a single slaying, from husband killers Mrs. Edith Carew and Ruth Synder to wife killers Adolph Luetgert and Dr. Bernard Finch.

In the following quizzes, the reader will undoubtedly pinpoint those killers whose spectacular acts brought them worldwide attention, taking note of personal peculiarities that are now fairly common knowledge, words and deeds that have become permanent entries in the lexicon of homicide.

QUIZ A

Score 5 points for each correct answer.

1. They murdered in pairs; match the murdering partners.

_____	1. Richard Loeb	**A.** Myron Lance
_____	2. William Burke	**B.** Perry Smith
_____	3. Richard Hickock	**C.** William Hare
_____	4. Walter Kelbach	**D.** Nathan Leopold
_____	5. Dean Corll	**E.** Elmer Henley

2. Match the American mass murderers with the number of victims credited to each.

_____	1. Jesse Pomeroy	**A.** 7
_____	2. Herman Webster Mudgett	**B.** 8
		C. 10
_____	3. Johann Otto Hoch	**D.** 13
_____	4. Richard Speck	**E.** 18
_____	5. Howard Unruh	**F.** 27
_____	6. Robert Benjamin Smith	**G.** 30
_____	7. Charles Starkweather	**H.** 32
		I. 50
_____	8. John Wayne Gacy	**J.** 200
_____	9. Charles Whitman	
_____	10. Belle Gunness	

3. Match the following mass murderers (from Europe, Asia, and South America) with the number of victims attributed to them.

_____ 1. Sawney Bean family   **A.** 30

_____ 2. Gilles de Rais   **B.** 32

_____ 3. Andreas Bichel   **C.** 40

_____ 4. Buhram   **D.** 50

_____ 5. Teofilo "Sparks"   **E.** 85
        Rojas
                     F. 610

_____ 6. Elizabeth Bathory   **G.** 800

_____ 7. Fritz Haarmann   **H.** 931

_____ 8. Bruno Ludke   **I.** 1,500

_____ 9. Carl Denke   **J.** 3,500

_____ 10. Burke and Hare

4. Match the American mass killer with the state in which he murdered.

_____ 1. Richard Speck   **A.** Texas

_____ 2. Charles   **B.** Illinois
        Starkweather
                     C. New Jersey

_____ 3. Howard Unruh   **D.** Arizona

_____ 4. Charles Whitman   **E.** Nebraska

_____ 5. Robert Benjamin
        Smith

5. Match the European mass killer with the country in which he or she murdered.

_____	**1.** Jean-Baptiste Troppmann	**A.**	Scotland
_____	**2.** Burke and Hare	**B.**	Germany
_____	**3.** Elizabeth Bathory	**C.**	France
_____	**4.** Sawney Bean family	**D.**	Hungary
_____	**5.** Fritz Haarmann	**E.**	England

6. Match the mass killer with his or her murder method.

_____	**1.** Buhram	**A.**	Poison
_____	**2.** H. H. Holmes	**B.**	Strangulation
_____	**3.** Charles Starkweather	**C.**	Knife
		D.	Gun
_____	**4.** Marie de Brinvilliers	**E.**	Suffocation
_____	**5.** Sawney Bean family		

7. Match the killer with his sobriquet.

_____	**1.** Fritz Haarmann	**A.**	"The Monster of Dusseldorf"
_____	**2.** Peter Kurten		
_____	**3.** Herman Webster Mudgett	**B.**	"The Cannibal"
		C.	"The Pied Piper of Tucson"
_____	**4.** Henri Desiré Landru	**D.**	"The Torture Doctor"
_____	**5.** Charles Schmid		
_____	**6.** Albert Fish	**E.**	"Bluebeard"
_____	**7.** Ralph Jerome Selz	**F.**	"The Laughing Killer"
		G.	"The Ogre of Hanover"

8. Match the killer with the type of victim he or she selected.

_____	**1.** Richard Speck	**A.** Children
_____	**2.** Earle Leonard Nelson	**B.** Sailors
_____	**3.** Harvey Murray Glatman	**C.** Young peasant girls
_____	**4.** Carl Panzram	**D.** Homosexual youths
_____	**5.** John Wayne Gacy	**E.** Landladies
_____	**6.** Burke and Hare	**F.** Nurses
_____	**7.** Elizabeth Bathory	**G.** Prospectors
_____	**8.** Alfred Packer	**H.** Female models
_____	**9.** Melvin David Rees	**I.** Spinsters
_____	**10.** Henri Desiré Landru	**J.** Women in cars

9. Match the killer with the movie based on his crime.

_____	**1.** Burke and Hare	**A.** _The Suspect_
_____	**2.** Henri Desiré Landru	**B.** _The Lodger_
_____	**3.** Robert Stroud	**C.** _In Cold Blood_
_____	**4.** Jack the Ripper	**D.** _Monsieur Verdoux_
_____	**5.** Richard Hickock and Perry Smith	**E.** _M_
_____	**6.** Peter Kurten	**F.** _The Birdman of Alcatraz_
_____	**7.** Dr. Hawley Harvey Crippen	**G.** _They Made Me a Criminal_
_____	**8.** Charles "Kid" McCoy	**H.** _Shadow of a Doubt_
_____	**9.** Earle Leonard Nelson	**I.** _The Flesh and the Fiends_

10. Match the killer with his or her victim.

_____	**1.** Winston Moseley	**A.**	Dr. Herman Tarnower
_____	**2.** Harry K. Thaw	**B.**	Albert Snyder
_____	**3.** Fitzhugh Coyle Goldsborough	**C.**	Sharon Tate
_____	**4.** Jean Harris	**D.**	William Marsh Rice
_____	**5.** Manson Family	**E.**	Kitty Genovese
_____	**6.** Henry Judd Gray	**F.**	Lisa Levy
_____	**7.** Theodore R. Bundy	**G.**	Mayor George Moscone
_____	**8.** Dan White	**H.**	Malcolm X
_____	**9.** Thomas Hagan	**I.**	Stanford White
_____	**10.** Albert T. Patrick	**J.**	David Graham Phillips

QUIZ B

The following statements are either true or false. Score 3 points for each correct answer.

1. America's first mass killer was Samuel Green, a New England brigand.   True or False?

2. One of the candidates for Jack the Ripper, Dr. Thomas Neill Cream, first served a prison term in Illinois for murder before departing for London. True or False?

3. The notorious Johann Otto Hoch specialized in killing pawnbrokers in the United States for decades. True or False?

4. Woman-murderer Landru kept extensive account books in which he recorded every article taken from his gullible victims.   True or False?

5. New York physician Robert Buckanan poisoned his wife in 1892 with morphine, then covered up the telltale signs by dropping belladonna in the dead woman's eyes.   True or False?

6. Mass slayer Charles Starkweather murdered the parents of his teenage sweetheart, Caril Fugate, because they had forbidden her to see him.   True or False?

7. Captain Charles I. Nash, who commanded the *Herbert Fuller,* went berserk while the ship was at sea and slaughtered his entire crew of nine.   True or False?

8. A sensational 1930 murder case involved an Amarillo, Texas, lawyer named A. D. Payne, who hanged his wife in a closet and left her body there for six months.   True or False?

9. Condemned New Orleans killer Kenneth Neu, a would-be singer, composed a song entitled "I'm Fit as a Fiddle and Ready to Hang," which he sang on the gallows.   True or False?

10. Martha Beck, the overweight lover of Raymond Fernandez, had nothing to do with the "Lonely Hearts" killings of the late 1940s and was railroaded to the chair, according to most experts. True or False?

11. Kidnap victim Bobbie Greenlease, Jr., was murdered by his abductors in New York. True or False?

12. Dr. Geza de Kaplany, who was convicted of the torture-murder of his beauty-queen wife in 1963, was paroled in 1976 so he could take up medical duties in Taiwan. True or False?

13. Mass killer Frederick W. Cowan of New Rochelle, New York, went berserk in 1977 because he could not stand the responsibilities of a promotion at the plant where he worked. True or False?

14. French mass slayer Gilles de Rais had once been the strong right arm of Joan of Arc. True or False?

15. The mad Hungarian countess Elizabeth Bathory killed young girls and bathed in their blood because she thought it would help her complexion. True or False?

16. The last words of convicted Indiana killer Steven T. Judy, executed on March 9, 1981, were: "I don't hold no grudges." True or False?

17. America's all-time mass murderer, H. H. Holmes, was a practicing surgeon. True or False?

18. John Wayne Gacy, Chicago mass murderer of the late 1970s, once had his picture taken with First Lady Rosalynn Carter. True or False?

19. Texas killer Charles Whitman once had his picture taken with President Lyndon Baines Johnson. True or False?

20. The solutions to almost all important murder cases solved by police stem from information supplied by informers. True or False?

QUIZ C

Score 4 points for each correct answer.

1. America's first (1847) murdering doctor was

   _____ **A.** Dr. Valorus P. Coolidge.

   _____ **B.** Dr. John White Webster.

   _____ **C.** Dr. Bennett Clarke Hyde.

2. Dr. Thomas Neill Cream, condemned poisoner of London prostitutes, yelled out a baffling unfinished statement a moment before he dropped through the trap. What were these haunting words?

   _____ **A.** "Jack the Ripper is _____"

   _____ **B.** "The Duke of Clarence performed _____"

   _____ **C.** "I am Jack _____"

3. The last words of mass murderer H. H. Holmes as he dropped through the trap in a Pennsylvania prison yard were:

   _____ **A.** "I didn't kill Minnie—Minnie killed—"

   _____ **B.** "You'll never find all the bodies!"

   _____ **C.** "Wait a minute—I forgot my prayers!"

4. Warren Waite, who killed his in-laws in a sensational New York case in 1916, was a practicing

   _____ **A.** concert violinist.

   _____ **B.** dentist.

   _____ **C.** ballet dancer.

5. Millionaire Harry K. Thaw murdered the famous architect Stanford White over the affections of

_____ **A.** Gay Gibson.

_____ **B.** Wanda Stopa.

_____ **C.** Evelyn Nesbit.

6. German mass slayer Fritz Haarmann not only murdered scores of young boys he picked up, but also

_____ **A.** sold their bodies to doctors for experiments.

_____ **B.** chopped up their bodies and sold the flesh as meat.

_____ **C.** sent the bodies to a wax museum for replicas to be made.

7. Robert Erler, who murdered a woman and child in Florida in 1968, was a

_____ **A.** mailman.

_____ **B.** editor.

_____ **C.** police officer.

8. Charles Starkweather's mass killing spree was later blamed on his resentment over the lowly job he held. What was his position?

_____ **A.** Sewer cleaner

_____ **B.** Garbage man

_____ **C.** Street sweeper

9. California slayer Harvey Murray Glatman enticed attractive young women to his home and murdered them under the guise of being a

_____ **A.** movie producer.

_____ **B.** record promoter.

_____ **C.** photographer.

10. Fitzhugh Coyle Goldsborough murdered novelist David Graham Phillips in 1911 in New York because he felt the author had

_____ **A.** maligned his socialite sister in his fiction.

_____ **B.** written too critically of his home town of Philadelphia.

_____ **C.** libeled his father.

11. Who was "The Boston Strangler"?

_____ **A.** Crawford Goldsby

_____ **B.** Matt Keimes

_____ **C.** Albert DeSalvo

12. Robert James, who had murdered several women for insurance, was finally tried and convicted of killing his last wife, Mary, in a bizarre fashion in 1935. What method did he employ?

_____ **A.** Put her leg in a box containing rattlesnakes

_____ **B.** Forced her to drink two gallons of castor oil

_____ **C.** Strapped dynamite to her chest while she was drugged and blew her up

13. The Indian mass killer Buhram belonged to a murder sect. What was its name?

_____ **A.** Ku Klux Klan

_____ **B.** Thuggee

_____ **C.** Sepoy Stranglers

14. Chester Gillette drowned his girlfriend Grace Brown in a New York lake in 1906. What famous novel did his case inspire?

_____ **A.** *The Great Gatsby*

_____ **B.** *An American Tragedy*

_____ **C.** *Beyond the Horizon*

15. Adolf Louis Luetgert found a unique way to dispose of his wife's body after murdering her, one that inspired a macabre song years later. What did this Chicago businessman do?

_____ **A.** He put the body in a sausage vat in his plant and boiled it down.

_____ **B.** He dumped the body in cement which became the cornerstone of the *Tribune* Tower.

_____ **C.** He chopped up the body and fed it to his hogs.

16. A stellar Hollywood personality was murdered in 1922, in a case that was never solved. Who was the victim?

_____ **A.** William Desmond Taylor

_____ **B.** Clara Bow

_____ **C.** Ralph Ince

17. In 1921 William A. Hightower, who later became a prison columnist, committed a particularly repugnant murder in San Francisco, which incensed the nation because his victim was a

_____ **A.** nun.

_____ **B.** priest.

_____ **C.** child.

18. Who was known as "The French Ripper" of the 1890s?

_____ **A.** Ludwig Tessov

_____ **B.** Alfred Deeming

_____ **C.** Joseph Vacher

19. He was a cannibal-murderer residing in Wisconsin and his case inspired the writing of the book *Psycho*. Who was he?

_____ **A.** Bart Caritativo

_____ **B.** Ed Gein

_____ **C.** Harry T. Hayward

20. His story and execution inspired Norman Mailer to write a ridiculously contrived book about him. What was this killer's name?

_____ **A.** Gary Gilmore

_____ **B.** Theodore Bundy

_____ **C.** Jesse Bishop

QUIZ D

Match the killer to his profile. Score 5 points for each correct answer.

1. Roland B. Molineux
2. Thomas Piper
3. Gerald Thompson
4. Martin Thorn
5. Charles Avinain
6. Jack Gilbert Graham
7. Harry T. Hayward
8. Vincenz Verzeni
9. George Chapman
10. Carl Otto Wanderer
11. Bela Kiss
12. Ernest Ingenito
13. Herbert Mullin
14. John Wayne Gacy
15. Richard Speck
16. Juan Corona
17. Frans Hooijaiers
18. William "Theo" Durrant
19. Charles Gibbs
20. Klaus Gossmann

_____ **A.** He worked as a construction contractor, lived in an upper-middle-class suburb of Chicago, and dressed up as a clown for children's parties and benefits. He was a well-liked neighbor and an ardent worker for the Democratic Party. At night he cruised around Chicago's "Bughouse Square" picking up homosexual prostitutes, whom he murdered by the score.

_____ **B.** A German college student, he killed and robbed at noontime, which won for him the sobriquet of "Midday Murderer." He planned to kidnap or kill actress Elke Sommer when she visited her home town of Nuremberg.

_____ **C.** An American pirate from Rhode Island, he led a mutiny on board the *Vineyard*, killing the captain and mate. Before he was hanged in 1831 he bragged of murdering more than four hundred people as a pirate, but his toll was probably about half that number.

_____ **D.** A wealthy member of New York's high society, he poisoned two persons in 1898, one by accident, because, as members of his private club, they displeased him. He died in an insane asylum.

_____ **E.** A petty criminal most of his life, in 1955 he planted a bomb aboard a Denver airplane in which his mother was traveling. The explosion killed forty-four people, and he immediately tried to collect the insurance he had taken out on his mother's life. He was caught by the FBI and sent to the gas chamber.

_____ **F.** He killed thirteen people; his drug-muddled mind produced a strange rationale for murder—he was killing people as a sacrifice to the gods in order to prevent California earthquakes.

_____ **G.** He worked as a sexton in a Boston church, waylaying women and children of the parish in 1873–74. Before his execution he stated: "I am a very bad man."

_____ **H.** A French mass murderer, he was a butcher by trade. He killed farmers and took their livestock. Before he was guillotined, he shouted: "Never confess!"

_____ **I.** He was an American hero of World War I who arranged for the murder of his wife in Chicago in 1920. He was exposed as a killer by Ben Hecht and Charles MacArthur, then the best police reporters in town.

_____ **J.** Migrant workers were his employees and his victims, twenty-five in all killed at his hands in California. He was sent to prison for life in 1973.

_____ **K.** A onetime monk, he became a male nurse in the Netherlands and began killing his patients by injection. He was convicted of murdering five invalids (the prosecution estimated the overall toll to be 259) and sentenced to thirteen years in prison.

_____ **L.** He murdered his girlfriend, Kitty Ging, in Minneapolis in 1894, after insuring her life. His last request before hanging was that the gallows be painted fire-engine red, his favorite color. His wish was granted.

_____ **M.** A professional thief and burglar, he claimed that he was in a drugged state when he killed eight women in Chicago in 1966.

_____ **N.** He was a mild-mannered toolmaker in Peoria, Illinois, but at night he busied himself with raping women, forcing them to lewdly pose before his camera in the glare of his car's headlights on lonely roads. He raped sixteen women and murdered his last sex victim before being caught. Asked how he felt after murdering Mildred Hallmark, he shrugged and said: "I slept like a baby." He went to the electric chair on October 15, 1935.

_____ **O.** A Hungarian tinsmith, this mass slayer first killed his wife, Maria, in 1912, along with her lover. On the promise of marriage he lured twenty-one women to his Budapest apartment, where he murdered them for their money. He secreted the bodies in huge barrels of alcohol outside his rural cottage before burying them. He entered the service during World War I and was never found.

_____ **P.** A petty burglar and sneak thief, he went berserk on the night of November 17, 1950, and shot eight persons, most of them his in-laws, killing seven. He was sent to an insane asylum in New Jersey for life.

_____ **Q.** Working as an assistant Sunday school teacher in San Francisco, he strangled and mutilated two young women of his parish in 1895, dragging their bodies to the tower of the Emanuel Baptist Church. He was not hanged for his crimes until 1898.

_____ **R.** After studying this mass killer's body, phrenologists concluded that his physical proportions typified him as a psychopathic killer. An Italian born in the slums of Rome, he is credited with slaying twelve women, drinking their blood like a fictional vampire.

_____ **S.** His New York landlady, Mrs. Augusta Nack, encouraged him to murder and dissect another tenant, Willie Guldensuppe, scattering the remains all around Manhattan in 1897. Mrs. Nack reportedly urged the murder because Guldensuppe refused to be part of a sex troika. The tenant went to the electric chair; Mrs. Nack got only ten years, and upon her release opened a delicatessen.

_____ **T.** His real name was Severin Klosowski; he migrated from Poland to London and promptly began poisoning women, mostly his wives, to obtain their savings. When he was arrested in 1902, many at Scotland Yard thought him to be Jack the Ripper, but the killer, hanged on April 7, 1903, employed a completely different modus operandi than the infamous Jack.

SCORING

Quiz A   _____

Quiz B   _____

Quiz C   _____

Quiz D   _____

     Chapter Total Score   _____

Your Homicide Squad Rating

If you scored between 620 and 430

You rank with the great Vidocq.

If you scored between 429 and 196

You can work for the Chicago P.D. any time.

If you scored between 195 and 0

Get out of those plain clothes.

THE

LAWMEN

THE

LAWMEN

From Wyatt Earp to J. Edgar Hoover in America and from Vidocq to the venerable inspectors of Scotland Yard, the lawman has had a hard lot, in that he has historically competed for public favor against the manufactured glamour of the criminal. Ironically, in his role of enforcing laws demanded by the public the lawman has become more reviled by the public than the criminal, treated almost like an enemy of the average citizen—almost like the criminal he is dedicated to apprehending on the public's behalf.

This paradoxical situation has created the image of the lawman as oppressor, or, at least, one outside the public's concept of popularity. Yet the lawman has brought greatness and compassion to his role of authority. He has proved himself the righteous rival to any criminal, and the stars of his profession are as immortal in memory as are his age-old nemeses. Let's see how well the reader can pinpoint the lawmen.

QUIZ A

Score 5 points for each correct answer.

1. Match the lawman with the actor and motion picture dealing with his career.

_____ 1. J. Edgar Hoover

_____ 2. Wyatt Earp

_____ 3. Joseph Petrosino

_____ 4. Wild Bill Hickok

_____ 5. Thomas E. Dewey

_____ 6. Pat Garrett

A. Gary Cooper in *The Plainsman*

B. Ernest Borgnine in *Pay or Die*

C. Addison Richards in *G-Men*

D. Burt Lancaster in *Gunfight at the O.K. Corral*

E. Thomas Mitchell in *The Outlaw*

F. Humphrey Bogart in *The Enforcer*

2. Match the lawman with the criminal he pursued.

_____ 1. J. Edgar Hoover

_____ 2. Joe Lefors

_____ 3. Wyatt Earp

_____ 4. Al Dewey

_____ 5. Eugène Vidocq

A. Butch Cassidy and the Sundance Kid

B. Clair Raoul

C. Richard Hickock and Perry Smith

D. Frank Stilwell

E. Alvin Karpis

3. Match the lawman with his organization.

_____	**1.** Melvin Purvis	**A.**	Texas Rangers
_____	**2.** Gustave Macé	**B.**	Scotland Yard
_____	**3.** Walter Dew	**C.**	Sûreté Générale
_____	**4.** John B. Armstrong	**D.**	Federal Bureau of Narcotics
_____	**5.** Harry Anslinger		
		E.	Federal Bureau of Investigation

4. Match the lawman with the city police department he commanded.

_____	**1.** Orlando Wilson	**A.**	Tombstone, Arizona
_____	**2.** Lewis Valentine		
_____	**3.** Sir Robert Peel	**B.**	London
_____	**4.** Wyatt Earp	**C.**	Chicago, Illinois
_____	**5.** Bat Masterson	**D.**	Dodge City, Kansas
		E.	New York City

5. Match the lawman with the criminal he shot it out with.

_____	**1.** Wild Bill Hickok	**A.**	Bill Doolin
_____	**2.** FBI	**B.**	Dave Tutt
_____	**3.** "T-Men"	**C.**	"Ma" and Fred Barker
_____	**4.** Heck Thomas		
_____	**5.** Danny Healy	**D.**	Vincent Drucci
		E.	Victor Lustig

QUIZ B

The following statements are either true or false. Score 3 points for each correct answer.

1. Matt Leach, captain of the Indiana State Police, who dogged the trail of John Dillinger, received in the mail a booklet entitled "How to Be a Detective," which Dillinger had ordered for him. True or False?

2. Sam Cowley, special agent of the FBI's Chicago office, shot and killed "Ma" Barker. True or False?

3. Vidocq, the first chief of France's Sûreté Générale, was an archcriminal before he began working for the law. True or False?

4. "Baby Face" Nelson shot and killed two FBI agents near Little Bohemia Lodge in 1934 during an abortive raid to capture the Dillinger gang. True or False?

5. J. Edgar Hoover, head of the FBI, personally arrested Alvin Karpis in New Orleans in 1936. True or False?

6. George Washington Matsell was the first Chief of Police in New York City. True or False?

7. British policemen were dubbed "Bobbies" after the force's founder, Sir Robert Peel. True or False?

8. Carlo Gambino, who became one of the five Mafia chieftains of New York, was originally a policeman. True or False?

9. Fritz Haarmann, who killed young wayward boys in Hanover by the score, was given a police badge as an informer by German authorities. True or False?

10. The detective arm of the London police is called the CID (Criminal Investigation Department). True or False?

QUIZ C

Score 4 points for each correct answer.

1. Alan Ladd played the title role of *Whispering Smith*, about a Western lawman. The character was based upon

    _____ **A.** Joe Lefors.

    _____ **B.** Chris Madsen.

    _____ **C.** Wyatt Earp.

2. Who really captured George "Machine Gun" Kelly in a Memphis rooming house in 1933?

    _____ **A.** FBI agents

    _____ **B.** W. J. Raney of the Memphis Police Department

    _____ **C.** Operatives of the Burns Detective Agency

3. The killing of Elizabeth Short in Los Angeles in 1947, known as "The Black Dahlia Case," is unsolved to this day. Who was the L.A. police detective who stayed with the case for decades?

_____ **A.** Harry L. Hansen

_____ **B.** Joseph Wambaugh

_____ **C.** Moroni Olsen

4. During the Jazz Age, America boasted two famous and unorthodox Prohibition agents. Who were they?

_____ **A.** Eliot Ness and Richard Canfield

_____ **B.** Moe Smith and Izzy Einstein

_____ **C.** Harry Daugherty and Jess Smith

5. Who was J. Edgar Hoover's predecessor as head of the FBI?

_____ **A.** Max Shinburn

_____ **B.** David Loring

_____ **C.** William J. Burns

6. In which country were the early-day police wagons first dubbed "Black Marias"?

_____ **A.** United States

_____ **B.** England

_____ **C.** Canada

7. The word "copper," from the copper buttons once worn on police uniforms, originated, circa 1846, in what country?

_____ **A.** England

_____ **B.** Australia

_____ **C.** United States

8. The slaughter of lawmen—two detectives, a police chief, and an FBI agent—in the Kansas City Massacre of 1933 was an abortive attempt to free gangster Frank "Jelly" Nash, who was in custody, and was killed in the barrage unleashed by the attackers. Who were the killers?

_____ **A.** Verne Miller, William "Solly" Weissman, and Maurice and Homer Denning

_____ **B.** Charles Arthur "Pretty Boy" Floyd and Adam Richetti

_____ **C.** George "Baby Face" Nelson and John Paul Chase

9. A dogged Philadelphia police detective tracked down the elusive mass killer H. H. Holmes (Herman Webster Mudgett) in 1894. Who was the sleuth?

_____ **A.** George Leonidas Leslie

_____ **B.** Eduardo Cianelli

_____ **C.** Frank P. Geyer

10. Master jewel thief John Arthur MacLean, who reportedly engineered robberies totaling more than $131 million, was tracked down by an undercover man of the Fort Lauderdale, Florida, police department in 1979. Who was this supercop?

_____ **A.** Leo Callahan

_____ **B.** Arthur McLellan

_____ **C.** Timothy Carey

QUIZ D

Match the lawman with his profile. Score 5 points for each correct answer.

1. Jim Amos	**7.** Jonathan Whicher
2. John Stege	**8.** William J. Burns
3. Alan Pinkerton	**9.** Melvin Purvis
4. Wild Bill Hickok	**10.** François Eugène Vidocq
5. J. Edgar Hoover	
6. Wyatt Earp	

_____ **A.** An incorruptible police captain in Chicago, he headed the special "Dillinger squad" all during the bank-robbing spree of the Hoosier bandit.

_____ **B.** Novelist Honoré de Balzac based his character Inspector Vautrin in *Le Père Goriot* upon this first of police detectives in the world. He was also to become Edgar Allan Poe's character Dupin.

_____ **C.** He sought the limelight in the early 1930s, setting himself up as a one-man crusade against gangsters, but for all his self-aggrandizing publicity, he proved inept and reckless. He was responsible for the raid against the Little Bohemia Lodge in April 1934, in which FBI agents shot and killed one innocent man and wounded two others in their attempt to capture the Dillinger gang. This overrated lawman committed suicide, it was later alleged.

_____ **D.** A supersleuth for Scotland Yard, this venerable Detective-Inspector ran afoul of sixteen-year-old Constance Kent, who murdered her brother. He alone believed the girl guilty, and he was pressured into early retirement only to be exonerated later when Constance confessed. He was portrayed as Sergeant Cuff in *The Moonstone* by Wilkie Collins.

_____ **E.** He once guarded President Theodore Roosevelt, and was appointed as an agent to the Bureau of Investigation in 1921, the first black in America to hold such a position.

_____ **F.** Known as "The Prince of Pistoleers" in the Old West, this sometime lawman was shot in the back by a drunken bindlestiff named Jack McCall. The lawman was playing cards at the time, his last cards being aces and eights, which have since been known as "the dead man's hand."

_____ **G.** His first important police job was guarding President Abraham Lincoln; he later founded a powerful detective agency, its logo showing a wide-staring eye and the words "We never sleep."

_____ **H.** Of all lawmen in the U.S., his name stood foremost in the public mind and eye, chiefly because he was an excellent promoter of that name. He was the ultimate bureaucrat, who inexplicably refused to admit to the existence of America's national crime syndicate until the twilight of his career. He preferred chasing "Reds."

_____ **I.** He headed the Bureau of Investigation but left his federal post in the glare of the Teapot Dome scandal. He formed a private detective agency that became famous across the country. His closest friend in England was Arthur Conan Doyle.

_____ **J.** As *the* legendary lawmen of the Old West, he and his brothers shot it out toe to toe with five outlaws in Tombstone, Arizona, in 1881; he lived to dictate his memoirs on the sunny porch of a California bungalow.

SCORING

Quiz A _____

Quiz B _____

Quiz C _____

Quiz D _____

   Chapter Total Score _____

Your Marshal Rating

If you scored between 250 and 171   Your gun cleaned up the West.

If you scored between 170 and 61   You've earned the name "copper."

If you scored between 60 and 0   You'd better think of turning in your badge.

MOUTHPIECES

MOUTHPIECES

The criminal lawyer—better known in movie argot as "the mouthpiece"—has provided high drama for courts, clients, and the public. His legalistic feats have been recorded by the press and the movies, which are undoubtedly responsible for the popular concept that lawyers, particularly criminal lawyers, are indispensable godlike figures without whose fiery presence in court the accused faces certain damnation.

Clever, ambitious, often self-serving to the point of disgusting displays of arrogance and defiance of the law itself, the breed of criminal lawyer has produced some of the most memorable personalities in the field of crime. The following quizzes will certainly jog the reader's memory in a roll call of famous (or infamous) mouthpieces.

QUIZ A

Score 5 points for each correct answer.

1. Match the criminal lawyer with his murder case.

_____ **1.** Clarence Darrow   **A.** Siegel-Greenburg Case

_____ **2.** Delphin Delmas

_____ **3.** Jerry Geisler   **B.** Thomas Massie Case

_____ **4.** Maître   **C.** Henri Landru Case
           Moro-Giafferi
                               D. Sam Sheppard Case
_____ **5.** F. Lee Bailey
                               E. Thaw-White Case

2. Match the criminal lawyer with his gangster client.

_____ **1.** Edward Bennett   **A.** Al Capone
           Williams
                               B. Charles "Lucky"
_____ **2.** Louis Piquett   Luciano

_____ **3.** J. Richard "Dixie" **C.** John Dillinger
           Davis
                               D. Vincent "Mad Dog"
_____ **4.** Charles Erbstein   Coll

_____ **5.** Moses Polakoff   **E.** Frank Costello

_____ **6.** Samuel Leibowitz   **F.** "Dutch" Schultz

3. Match the criminal lawyer with his notorious female client.

_____ **1.** William Kunstler   **A.** LaVerne Borelli

_____ **2.** Jake Ehrlich   **B.** Joanne Chesimard

_____ **3.** Samuel Leibowitz   **C.** Marie Lafarge

_____ **4.** George D. Robinson   **D.** Cecilia Cooney

        E. Lizzie Borden

_____ **5.** Charles Lachaud

4. Match the criminal lawyer with his or her rape case.

_____ **1.** Jerry Geisler   **A.** Scottsboro Case

_____ **2.** Samuel Leibowitz   **B.** Errol Flynn Case

_____ **3.** Garvin McNab   **C.** Doris McCarthy Case

_____ **4.** Gladys Towles Root   **D.** Arbuckle-Rappe Case

5. Match the criminal lawyer with the motion picture dealing with his life or one of his most important cases.

_____ **1.** Clarence Darrow   **A.** _The Girl in the Red Velvet Swing_

_____ **2.** Delphin Delmas

_____ **3.** Maître Moro-Gaifferi   **B.** _Inherit the Wind_

        C. _Crime Without Passion_

_____ **4.** William Fallon

_____ **5.** Charles Erbstein   **D.** _Party Girl_

        E. _Bluebeard_

QUIZ B

The following statements are either true or false. Score 3 points for each correct answer.

1. Earl Rogers defended Clarence Darrow against jury-bribing charges stemming from the bombing of the *Los Angeles Times* in 1910, a Darrow case.   True or False?

2. Vincent Bugliosi, later a distinguished trial lawyer, prosecuted the murder cultist Charles Manson. True or False?

3. Clarence Darrow was a native of Georgia, where his law offices were permanently located.   True or False?

4. Dr. John Hill, in a sensational Texas murder case, was defended by Richard "Racehorse" Haynes. True or False?

5. The famous admonition to clients to "never plead guilty" originated with Jake Ehrlich.   True or False?

6. As a rule of law, in murder trials *corpus delicti* means the body of a homicide victim.   True or False?

7. At Steinie Morrison's controversial murder trial in England he was defended by Edward Abinger, whose unorthodox methods almost ruined his career.   True or False?

8. Charles Lachaud, France's leading criminal lawyer of the nineteenth century, defended the notorious blackmailer Jeanne Brécourt.   True or False?

9. In American jurisprudence, Massachusetts, in 1866, was the first state to make the accused a competent witness. True or False?

10. Criminal lawyer William F. Fallon secretly drank in court, purposely intoxicating himself when defending his chief client, Arnold Rothstein, whom he hated. True or False?

QUIZ C

Score 4 points for each correct answer.

1. Which of the following criminal lawyers wrote the book *My Life in Court*?

   _____ A. Louis Nizer

   _____ B. Alfred Julien

   _____ C. Vincent Hallinan

2. Which criminal attorney was known as "The Great Mouthpiece"?

   _____ A. Charles Erbstein

   _____ B. William Fallon

   _____ C. Delphin Delmas

3. Fiery New York District Attorney William Travers Jerome prosecuted a famous criminal lawyer. Who was he?

   _____ A. Abraham Hummel

   _____ B. William Howe

   _____ C. Earl Rogers

4. Mass killer Theodore Bundy was defended in a 1979 murder trial by which lawyer?

_____ **A.** Gladys Towles Root

_____ **B.** Jane Darwell

_____ **C.** Margaret Good

5. Percy Foreman defended which of the following killers?

_____ **A.** Lee Harvey Oswald

_____ **B.** James Earl Ray

_____ **C.** Charles Whitman

_____ **D.** All of the above

6. F. Lee Bailey defended which of the following killers?

_____ **A.** Juan Corona

_____ **B.** Herbert Mullin

_____ **C.** Albert DeSalvo

_____ **D.** All of the above

7. Melvin Belli defended which of the following killers?

_____ **A.** Sirhan Sirhan

_____ **B.** Jack Ruby

_____ **C.** John Wayne Gacy

_____ **D.** All of the above

8. Edward J. Reilly, who led the defense of kidnapper Bruno Richard Hauptmann in 1935,

_____ A. lost the case, with Hauptmann being condemned.

_____ B. managed to get his client a suspended sentence.

_____ C. won an acquittal based on legal technicalities.

9. The first of two sensational murder trials of Texas multimillionaire oilman T. Cullen Davis was brought to a shocking acquittal by

_____ A. Percy Foreman.

_____ B. F. Lee Bailey.

_____ C. Richard "Racehorse" Haynes.

10. Nicola Sacco and Bartolomeo Vanzetti were defended at the onset of their world-famous trial in 1921 by

_____ A. the same lawyer.

_____ B. separate lawyers.

_____ C. two lawyers each.

QUIZ D

Match the criminal lawyer with his profile. Score five points for each correct answer.

1. Clarence Darrow
2. William Fallon
3. William Kunstler
4. Abraham Hummel
5. Jake Ehrlich

_____ **A.** He was the most flamboyant attorney for gangsters in the 1920s, representing Arnold Rothstein and Nicky Arnstein, Fannie Brice's errant husband. A drinker and raconteur, he was addicted to Broadway showgirls and the company of writers.

_____ **B.** No criminal lawyer before or since in America practiced such unscrupulous methods as this man. With his partner, William Howe, this attorney thought nothing of bribing a judge, blackmailing a jurist, perjuring a witness. From 1869 to 1907 he represented the worst of the underworld, including Fredericka "Marm" Mandelbaum, and Edward S. Stokes, murderer of "Big Jim" Fisk.

_____ **C.** A California powerhouse of criminal law, he was the legal guardian angel of moviedom, defending film stars and entertainment celebrities such as drummer Gene Krupa and singer Billie Holiday on drug charges.

_____ **D.** More of a crusader for human rights than a practicing attorney, he defended "Big Bill" Haywood and the Wobblies, and a lonely teacher named Scopes.

_____ **E.** To this day he is generally known as a defender of archliberal causes, chiefly political. He was the chief counsel for the notorious "Chicago Seven," defendants placed on trial for demonstrations against the 1968 Democratic Convention in Chicago.

SCORING

Quiz A   _____

Quiz B   _____

Quiz C   _____

Quiz D   _____

   Chapter Total Score   _____

Your Defense Counsel Rating

**If you scored
between 220 and 146**   No case is hopeless in your hands.

**If you scored
between 145 and 66**   Your advice to F. Lee Bailey will be
                             cherished.

**If you scored
between 65 and 0**   Sit in the spectators' section and
                             take notes.

THE

OUTLAWS

THE

OUTLAWS

Those pioneers of the early West who made their living from their ability to use a six-gun were essentially pretty low characters, not the nobly-inclined stereotypes in our movie and TV fare dealing with Western badmen. They killed not in high-noon stand-up battles but as back-shooters cowering in shadowy alleys for the most part. Even lawmen of the era were a conniving sort. Wyatt Earp was an exception. So, too, were Wild Bill Hickok, Bill Tilghman, Heck Thomas, and Chris Madsen. Most lawmen were more like Tom Horn and Dallas Stoudenmire—marshals of the law one minute, killers for hire the next.

The true badmen, whom the reader will certainly recognize in the following quizzes, were generally illiterate, immoral, and unwashed, a foul-smelling lot scrubbed down by the fiction of Zane Grey and Owen Wister. Yet, from Jesse James to Billy the Kid, they were always fascinating and unforgettable, no matter what their crimes.

QUIZ A

Score 5 points for each correct answer.

1. Match the outlaw with the actor and motion picture based on his career.

_____ 1. Billy the Kid

_____ 2. Jesse James

_____ 3. Frank James

_____ 4. Doc Holliday

_____ 5. Cole Younger

_____ 6. Bob Ford

_____ 7. John Wesley Hardin

_____ 8. Ike Clanton

  A. Jason Robards, Jr., in *Hour of the Gun*

  B. Paul Newman in *The Left-Handed Gun*

  C. Robert Duvall in *The Great Northfield, Minnesota, Raid*

  D. Wendell Corey in *The Great Missouri Raid*

  E. John Ireland in *I Shot Jesse James*

  F. Rock Hudson in *The Lawless Breed*

  G. Robert Ryan in *Hour of the Gun*

  H. Alan Hale, Jr., in *The True Story of Jesse James*

2. Match the outlaws who rode together.

_____	**1.** James Brothers	**A.** McLowery Brothers
_____	**2.** Belle Starr	**B.** Sundance Kid
_____	**3.** Butch Cassidy	**C.** Blue Duck
_____	**4.** Bill Doolin	**D.** Younger Brothers
_____	**5.** Clanton Brothers	**E.** Dalton Brothers

3. The last great outlaw band of the West was called "The Wild Bunch." Match the members of this outlaw brotherhood with their sobriquets.

_____	**1.** Ben Kilpatrick	**A.** "Butch Cassidy"
_____	**2.** William Carver	**B.** "Dixon"
_____	**3.** Harvey Logan	**C.** "Sundance Kid"
_____	**4.** George L. Curry	**D.** "Camilla"
_____	**5.** Harry Tracy	**E.** "Peg Leg"
_____	**6.** Frank Elliot	**F.** "Mad Dog"
_____	**7.** O. C. Hanks	**G.** "Flat Nose"
_____	**8.** Harry Longabaugh	**H.** "Kid Curry"
_____	**9.** Will Roberts	**I.** "News"
_____	**10.** Robert Leroy Parker	**J.** "The Tall Texan"

4. Match the badman of the West with the lawman who tracked him down.

_____	**1.** Bill Doolin	**A.** Pat Garrett
_____	**2.** Billy the Kid	**B.** Wyatt Earp
_____	**3.** Billy Clanton	**C.** Wild Bill Hickok
_____	**4.** John Wesley Hardin	**D.** Heck Thomas
_____	**5.** Dave Tutt	**E.** John Selman

5. The outlaws roamed the Western states, robbing at will, but were identified with specific states. Match the outlaws with the states considered their territory of operations.

_____	**1.** Sam Bass	**A.** Kansas
_____	**2.** Butch Cassidy	**B.** Texas
_____	**3.** Jesse James	**C.** Oklahoma
_____	**4.** Black Bart	**D.** Missouri
_____	**5.** Bill Doolin	**E.** Colorado
_____	**6.** Dalton Brothers	**F.** California

6. There were many "Bills" in the Old West. Match the outlaw with his sobriquet.

_____	**1.** William Brocius	**A.** "Old Bill"
_____	**2.** William Miner	**B.** "Cherokee Bill"
_____	**3.** Crawford Goldsby	**C.** "Billy the Kid"
_____	**4.** William Jones	**D.** "Little Bill"
_____	**5.** William Raidler	**E.** "Canada Bill"
_____	**6.** William Bonney	**F.** "Curly Bill"

7. "Dicks" and "Blacks" were also numerous in the outlaw era. Match the outlaw with his sobriquet.

_____	**1.** Dan Clifton	**A.** "Black Bart"
_____	**2.** Richard West	**B.** "Dynamite Dick"
_____	**3.** Charles E. Bolton	**C.** "Little Dick"
_____	**4.** Thomas Ketchum	**D.** "Rattlesnake Dick"
_____	**5.** Richard Barter	**E.** "Black Jack"

QUIZ B

The following statements are either true or false. Score 3 points for each correct answer.

1. The Apache Kid was a sergeant of scouts on the San Carlos Reservation in New Mexico before turning renegade and murderer.   True or False?

2. Rufus Buck and his gang terrorized southern Kansas in a robbery-rape spree in 1895.   True or False?

3. Jesse James was a kindhearted robber, exactly as the legends about him claimed, never really taking a life in his long career as an outlaw.   True or False?

4. Frank James was a sanctimonious Bible-reading man who quoted scripture to cover up his outlaw image. True or False?

5. George "Red Buck" Weightman and George "Bitter Creek" Newcomb were members of the Doolin Gang. True or False?

6. Rube and Jim Burrow, who robbed trains in Arkansas and Texas in the late 1880s, were both pardoned and lived out their lives as Hollywood stunt men during the era of silent movies.   True or False?

7. Al Jennings was one of the most successful bandits of the Old West, who lived out a life of ease with the fortunes he took from trains and banks.   True or False?

8. Grat Dalton was the only surviving member of the Dalton gang following its abortive raid in Coffeeville, Kansas, in 1892.   True or False?

9. The first bank robbery in the U.S. was not by outlaw Jesse James and his band but by Edward W. Green, who robbed the Malden (Massachusetts) Bank on December 15, 1863.   True or False?

10. Gunfighter John Wesley Hardin studied law for years while in prison and became a lawyer when released.   True or False?

QUIZ C

Score 4 points for each correct answer.

1. Who was the "dirty little coward" who shot and killed Jesse James?

    _____ A. Dick Liddell

    _____ B. Charlie Clements

    _____ C. Bob Ford

    _____ D. Cole Younger

2. Which outlaw band of brothers is credited with the first train robbery in America?

_____ **A.** James Brothers

_____ **B.** Farrington Brothers

_____ **C.** Dalton Brothers

_____ **D.** Reno Brothers

3. Who was the outlaw who, after being captured along with his two brothers, all terribly wounded in a shoot-out with a Minnesota posse, told reporters: "We are victims of circumstances. We was drove to it, sir!"

_____ **A.** Grat Dalton

_____ **B.** George Sontag

_____ **C.** Cole Younger

_____ **D.** Rube Burrow

4. This Texas outlaw died on July 19, 1878, shot during a holdup. His last words were: "Let me go—the world is bobbing around!" Who was he?

_____ **A.** Billy the Kid

_____ **B.** Sam Bass

_____ **C.** Sam Starr

_____ **D.** Al Spencer

5. Who was called the "Hanging Judge" of the Old West?

_____ **A.** Judge Isaac Parker

_____ **B.** Judge Roy Bean

_____ **C.** Judge Kenesaw Mountain Landis

6. What outlaw is considered to this day to have been the fastest gun in the Old West?

_____ **A.** John Wesley Hardin

_____ **B.** Clay Allison

_____ **C.** Ben Thompson

7. Which of the outlaws who rode with Jesse James on the disastrous raid against Northfield, Minnesota, banks in 1876 was killed?

_____ **A.** Clell Miller

_____ **B.** Bill Chadwell

_____ **C.** Charlie Pitts

_____ **D.** All of the above

8. Which Texas gunfighter reportedly killed thirty men and was hanged at Giddings, Texas, saying, while the rope was placed about his neck: "I deserve this fate. It is a debt I owe for a wild and reckless life. So long, everybody!"

_____ **A.** Clay Allison

_____ **B.** Joseph "Rowdy Joe" Lowe

_____ **C.** William P. Longley

9. Who was the outlaw who robbed his first stagecoach in California in 1869 and held up a train in White Sulphur, Georgia, in 1911, a forty-two-year span of robbery?

_____ **A.** "Old Bill" Miner

_____ **B.** Joaquin Murieta

_____ **C.** John Murrel

10. Who were the outlaws killed by the Earp Brothers and Doc Holliday in the Gunfight at the O.K. Corral in Tombstone, Arizona, in 1881?

_____ **A.** Tom McLowery

_____ **B.** Frank McLowery

_____ **C.** Billie Clanton

_____ **D.** Billy Claiborne

_____ **E.** All of the above

QUIZ D

Match the outlaw with his profile. Score 5 points for each correct answer.

1. Jesse James
2. John Wesley Hardin
3. Clay Allison
4. Butch Cassidy
5. Joaquin Murieta
6. Younger Brothers
7. Ben Thompson
8. Dalton Brothers
9. Tom Horn
10. "Black Jack" Ketchum

_____ **A.** He was a lawman and a onetime Pinkerton detective who hired himself out as an assassin and was eventually hanged (with the very rope he made while in his prison cell), after drunkenly confessing his murders to lawman Joe Lefors.

_____ **B.** He was one of the most ruthless killers of the Old West; his robbing career spanned eighteen years. Following his death he was immediately lionized as a folk hero, and he is remembered as such to this day.

_____ **C.** An alcoholic killer, this New Mexico gunslinger reportedly shot down fifteen men before falling dead drunk from his wagon in 1887 and being killed as a wheel rolled over his neck.

_____ **D.** Born in Missouri, these brothers robbed trains and banks in Oklahoma and along the Cherokee Strip, but they met disaster in Coffeyville, Kansas, in 1892, when they were shot while attempting to rob two banks. One brother survived to write a best-seller about the gang's escapades.

_____ **E.** Born in England, he migrated to the U.S. as a child and served in the Texas cavalry during the Civil War. He became a fast gun in Texas, with a dozen victims credited to him. He was killed in a San Antonio theater in 1884.

_____ **F.** Missouri-born, these brothers robbed banks and trains in seven states for almost twenty years before being captured. The oldest, who was the leader, survived to run a small Wild West show with Frank James.

_____ **G.** A New Mexico train robber, he was hanged in Clayton, New Mexico, in 1901, shouting from the gallows moments before he died: "I'll be in hell before you start breakfast, boys! Let her rip!"

_____ **H.** By his own count, he killed forty men in gun-fights before he was given a long prison term. Upon his release he moved to El Paso, Texas. He was shooting dice in a bar there in 1895 when he was killed, shot in the back. His last words, to a bartender, were: "Four sixes to beat!"

_____ **I.** His background is hazy, but it is known that he robbed gold miners and stages in California with ease. After a thousand-dollar reward was posted for him, dead or alive, a Texas Ranger named Harry Love appeared with a head in a bottle, which he claimed was that of the wanted outlaw. Great crowds assembled to view the grisly contents of the bottle, which had been put on display in Stockton, California, on June 24, 1853. The true fate of the outlaw remains a mystery to this day.

_____ **J.** He was the most affable of bank and train robbers, always disdaining to use his six-shooter, and leading a band of outlaws that hid out in a place called Hole-in-the-Wall. He reportedly traveled to South America and was killed while robbing a bank in Bolivia. His sister, however, maintained to her dying day that he returned to the U.S. and lived out a long life in obscurity, dying in Johnie, Nevada, in 1937.

SCORING

Quiz A   _____

Quiz B   _____

Quiz C   _____

Quiz D   _____

   Chapter Total Score   _____

Your Gunfighter Rating

If you scored between 353 and 246
John Wesley Hardin would walk across the street when you approached.

If you scored between 245 and 111
Your aim is accurate though your draw is a bit slow.

If you scored between 110 and 0
Get out of Dodge on the morning stage.

PRISONS

AND

PRISONERS

PRISONS

AND

PRISONERS

The prison and the prisoner have long been the subject of novels and motion pictures, from Dumas's *Count of Monte Cristo* to *Escape from Alcatraz,* firing the imagination of the public around the world. In reality, prison provides a dull, drab, and wearisome existence, an iron-gray world absent of hope. For the most part, inmates busy themselves with petty schemes that have nothing to do with heroic efforts to escape but center on obtaining better food and creature comforts, not to mention the development of abnormal sex practices.

There have been notable exceptions who have rebelled against prison systems, still archaic and inhuman around the world today. Penologists have studied these rare individuals as one would contemplate a strange breed of wild animal born in a zoo, wondering clinically about its chance for survival.

The following quizzes deal then with the exceptions in prison, inmates who achieved great notoriety before going behind bars—prisoners (and their wardens) who should spark the memory of the reader.

QUIZ A

Score 5 points for each correct answer.

1. Match the prisoner with the motion picture dealing with his prison life or escape.

_____	1. Robert Stroud	A. *Brute Force*
_____	2. John Wesley Hardin	B. *Cell 2455 Death Row*
_____	3. Joseph Paul Cretzer	
_____	4. Arthur "Dock" Barker	C. *White Heat*
		D. *The Lawless Breed*
_____	5. Caryl Chessman	E. *The Birdman of Alcatraz*

2. Match the infamous inmate with the prison in which he was last held prisoner.

_____	1. Al Capone	A. Leavenworth
_____	2. George "Machine Gun" Kelly	B. Alcatraz
		C. Eastham (Texas) Prison Farm
_____	3. John Dillinger	
_____	4. Clyde Barrow	D. Statesville (Illinois) Prison
_____	5. Roger Touhy	
		E. Michigan City (Indiana) State Prison

3. Match the prison argot with the meaning of each word.

_____	**1.** Screw	**A.**	Prison
_____	**2.** Stir	**B.**	Solitary confinement
_____	**3.** Hole		
_____	**4.** Max	**C.**	Escape
_____	**5.** Beat	**D.**	Guard
		E.	The full sentence under law

4. Match the warden with his famous prison.

_____	**1.** Lewis M. Lawes	**A.**	Joliet
_____	**2.** Tom White	**B.**	San Quentin
_____	**3.** Clinton Duffy	**C.**	Leavenworth
_____	**4.** Joseph E. Ragen	**D.**	Alcatraz
_____	**5.** E. B. Swope	**E.**	Sing Sing

5. Match the famous European prison with its country.

_____	**1.** Broadmoor	**A.**	Russia
_____	**2.** Santé	**B.**	England
_____	**3.** Lubianka	**C.**	Germany
_____	**4.** Spandau	**D.**	Ireland
_____	**5.** Kilmainham	**E.**	France

6. Match the prisoner with the jail, prison, or penal colony from which he escaped.

_____	**1.** John Dillinger	**A.**	Cayenne Penal Colony
_____	**2.** Eddie Guerin		
_____	**3.** Frank Nash	**B.**	Leavenworth
_____	**4.** Theodore Cole	**C.**	Lima (Ohio) Jail
_____	**5.** Harvey Bailey	**D.**	Alcatraz
		E.	Kansas State Penitentiary

QUIZ B

The following statements are either true or false. Score 3 points for each correct answer.

1. Arthur "Dock" Barker was killed while attempting to escape from Alcatraz in 1939.   True or False?

2. John Dillinger escaped from the "escape-proof" Indiana jail at Crown Point in 1934 by using a wooden gun.   True or False?

3. Dillinger stole the car belonging to Sheriff Lillian Holley, the fastest car in town, in his Crown Point escape.   True or False?

4. Henri Landru, the infamous "Bluebeard," escaped twice from prison but returned voluntarily to be executed.   True or False?

5. No one has ever successfully escaped from Alcatraz during the entire history of "The Rock" as a maximum-security prison.   True or False?

6. Robert Stroud, an inmate celebrity of Alcatraz, became world-famous for his experiments on rodents.   True or False?

7. Three men escaped from San Quentin in 1979 in a homemade kayak, the tower guards actually waving to them, thinking them boaters on an excursion. True or False?

8. Dale Otto Remling escaped from the Southern Michigan State Prison at Jackson in 1975 via helicopter, much like the escape depicted in the Charles Bronson motion picture *Breakout*.   True or False?

9. The largest mass prison escape in American history occurred in 1864, when the entire population of San Quentin broke loose and hundreds of felons battled posses to the death.   True or False?

10. Albert Fish, executed at Sing Sing in 1936 for child murder, had inserted so many needles in his body as a form of self-punishment that he actually short-circuited the electric chair.   True or False?

QUIZ C

Score 4 points for each correct answer.

1. Who were the two Chicago gangsters who were sentenced to serve long terms in the Cook County (Chicago) Jail during Prohibition but were allowed by a corrupt sheriff to leave the jail during the day to conduct their rackets?

    _____ **A.** Myles and Klondike O'Donnell

    _____ **B.** Terry Druggan and Frankie Lake

    _____ **C.** Albert Anselmi and John Scalise

2. What youthful outlaw of the Old West escaped from the jail in Mesilla, New Mexico, in 1881?

    _____ **A.** Clay Allison

    _____ **B.** John Wesley Hardin

    _____ **C.** William "Billy the Kid" Bonney

3. A bank robber with a sense of humor escaped from the State Hospital for the Criminally Insane at Matteawan, New York, in 1895, leaving the following note for startled guards:

    I don't intend to serve this out
    Or even let despair,
    Deprive me of my liberty
    Or give me one gray hair.

    Who was this felonious funnyman?

    _____ **A.** Cole Younger

    _____ **B.** Lloyd Barker

    _____ **C.** Oliver Curtis Perry

4. A convicted murderer, he wrote and published a regular newsletter from his San Quentin prison cell. Who was this notorious prisoner?

_____ A. Herbert Repsold

_____ B. William A. Hightower

_____ C. Ad Arkeley

5. The last of Butch Cassidy's "Wild Bunch" made a desperate escape from the Colorado State Prison in 1902, which resulted in a five-state manhunt for him; he committed suicide when a posse cornered him. What was his name?

_____ A. Dave Lant

_____ B. Harry Tracy

_____ C. Ben Kilpatrick

6. Nineteen men were led by a tough inmate in an escape from Ivy Bluff (North Carolina) Prison in 1959. Name the escape leader.

_____ A. Ralph Wood

_____ B. Roy Drake

_____ C. Charles "Yank" Stewart

7. Name the convict(s) involved with the prison break from Alcatraz in 1962, an escape which dispelled the belief that "The Rock" was escape-proof and led to the closing down of the prison.

_____ A. Joseph Anglin

_____ B. Frank Lee Morris

_____ C. Clarence Anglin

_____ D. All of the above

8. James Earl Ray, the convicted killer of Martin Luther King, Jr., made a sensational prison escape in 1977, which led to a six-state manhunt. From what prison did Ray escape?

   _____ **A.** Bridgewater State Mental Prison in Massachusetts

   _____ **B.** Missouri State Penitentiary

   _____ **C.** Brushy Mountain State Prison in Kentucky

9. Select the hardened convict(s) who accompanied Roger "The Terrible" Touhy in his sensational 1934 escape from Statesville Prison in Illinois.

   _____ **A.** Basil "The Owl" Banghart

   _____ **B.** Eugene O'Connor

   _____ **C.** St. Clair McInerney

   _____ **D.** All of the above

10. He engineered a mass prison break from the Michigan City (Indiana) State Prison in 1934 by smuggling guns to ten inmates inside a barrel of thread. Who was this master escape planner?

    _____ **A.** John Dillinger

    _____ **B.** Frank Nash

    _____ **C.** Wilbur Underhill

QUIZ D

Match the prison inmate with his profile. Score 5 points for each correct answer.

1. Robert Elliott Burns

2. Al Capone

3. Alfred Dreyfus

4. Alvin Karpis

5. Morris "Red" Rudensky

6. Jesse Pomeroy

7. Harvey Bailey

8. Stephen Dennison

9. Robert Stroud

10. Willie "The Actor" Sutton

_____ **A.** He was sent to Alcatraz from the federal penitentiary in Atlanta. At first he attempted to exercise control over other prisoners, pretending to be the boss he had been when free, but he was ignored and beaten, becoming docile and then somewhat mad—he suffered from paresis of the brain, brought on by syphilis. He was released in 1939, dying a raving lunatic in Florida in 1947.

_____ **B.** Sent to a New York reformatory in 1925 at age sixteen for stealing a five-dollar box of candy, this hapless inmate, a modern Jean Valjean, had years and years added to his sentence for small infractions without having committed a serious crime. He was kept in prison until 1959; he sued the state of New York for his thirty-four years behind bars and won $115,000, plus an apology.

_____ **C.** A mass killer of twenty-seven Boston area youths, he was sent to prison in 1881. Nine years later he discovered a broken gas pipe in his cell and attempted to blow himself out of his cell in a weird escape attempt by putting a lighted match to the gas. He was blown free of the cell but he was knocked unconscious, and the resulting fire killed three other inmates. He died in prison in 1932.

_____ **D.** A starving World War I veteran, he burglarized a store, taking $5.29, for which he was sent to a Georgia chain gang. He escaped, moving to Chicago, where he held a $20,000-a-year editor's job until he was turned in to Georgia authorities and returned to the chain gang. Again he escaped, fleeing to New Jersey, where he wrote a best-seller, *I Am a Fugitive from a Georgia Chain Gang*, which was later made into a smash movie with Paul Muni. Despite every effort by Georgia authorities to have him extradited, New Jersey officials refused to give up this escaped prisoner; he died a free man in 1955.

_____ **E.** He was the most successful burglar and safecracker of the 1920s, often in prison. He escaped from Leavenworth inside a small magazine box and was shipped by freight car from the prison, but he was placed upside down and hemorrhaged, the escaping blood giving him away. He totally reformed upon his release, becoming a consultant for the 3M Company regarding the manufacture of the firm's locks.

_____ **F.** One of the most spectacular bank robbers of the era, he was also known for his imaginative prison escapes: from Sing Sing in 1932, from Eastern State Penitentiary in 1945, and from Holmesburg Prison in Philadelphia in 1947. He later penned a best-seller, *Where the Money Was.*

_____ **G.** Imprisoned in 1909, he held the American record for the longest period of time spent in solitary confinement—forty-six years. He wrote *The Digest of Bird Diseases,* which became the definitive book on the subject.

_____ **H.** Unjustly accused of being a traitor, he was stripped of his military rank, publicly humiliated, and sent to the most feared prison in the world, Devil's Island. Not until the great French novelist and journalist Emile Zola wrote an immortal series of newspaper articles entitled "I Accuse" was the prisoner's case reopened. He was finally exonerated and returned to his position in the French army.

_____ **I.** He was a veteran bank robber of the 1920s who escaped from the Kansas State Penitentiary in 1933. He was captured following his break and locked up in the Dallas jail, from which he escaped days later; a deputy guard, Thomas Manion, gave him a hacksaw and helped him saw his way out. He was recaptured in Oklahoma and sent to Leavenworth for life for the kidnapping of Charles Urschel—a crime in which he had had no part. He was paroled in 1965 and lived out his life as a cabinetmaker in Joplin, Missouri, dying at ninety-one in 1979.

_____ **J.** For all his vaunted self-image as a tough bank robber, he was a cowardly sneak thief, according to his fellow inmates at Alcatraz, a raving homosexual who had been the lover of Fred Barker of the notorious Barker gang.

SCORING

Quiz A   _____

Quiz B   _____

Quiz C   _____

Quiz D   _____

   Chapter Total Score   _____

Your Warden Rating

If you scored between 270 and 196   You should be running Sing Sing.

If you scored between 195 and 86   The cons respect if not fear you.

If you scored between 85 and 0   Never step into the yard.

THE

SYNDICATE

THE

SYNDICATE

The forming of a national crime syndicate in the late 1920s produced the most sinister criminal intrusion into world society to date, the activities of its members woven into the fabric of everyday life, its take gleaned not only from the sale of illegal drugs, prostitution, and gambling, but from soiled restaurant tablecloths and drugstore vending machines.

Though the operations of the syndicate today are mostly concealed behind layers of legitimate businesses, its founders and charter members, a few still alive, were very much in yesterday's limelight and still emerge, as do their successors, into the glare of today's crime probes. The reader will now be tested in the following quizzes as he or she visualizes the sinister images that have flitted across motion picture and TV screens for the past fifty years.

QUIZ A

Score 5 points for each correct answer.

1. The first gangster enclave, meeting to form the national crime cartel, occurred at the Hotel President in Atlantic City in 1929. Match the gang leader with the city he represented.

_____ **1.** Al Capone	**A.** Newark, New Jersey
_____ **2.** Frank Costello	**B.** Philadelphia
_____ **3.** Charles "King" Solomon	**C.** New York
_____ **4.** Abner "Longy" Zwillman	**D.** Chicago
_____ **5.** Harry "Nig Rosen" Stromberg	**E.** Providence, Rhode Island
_____ **6.** Daniel Walsh	**F.** Boston

2. Match the member of the syndicate with his sobriquet.

_____ **1.** Joseph Bonanno

_____ **2.** Vincent Alo

_____ **3.** Tony Accardo

_____ **4.** Charles Gioe

_____ **5.** Albert Anastasia

_____ **6.** Frank Costello

_____ **7.** Joseph Aiuppa

_____ **8.** Felix Anthony Alderisio

_____ **9.** Joe Adonis

_____ **10.** Paul Ricca

A. "The Waiter"

B. "Big Tuna"

C. "The Prime Minister"

D. "Joey A"

E. "Milwaukee Phil"

F. "Mourning Doves"

G. "Lord High Executioner"

H. "Jimmy Blue Eyes"

I. "Joe Bananas"

J. "Cherry Nose"

3. Match the syndicate gangster with the motion picture dealing with his career.

_____ **1.** Vito Genovese

_____ **2.** Louis Buchalter

_____ **3.** Lucky Luciano

_____ **4.** Johnny Lazia

_____ **5.** Ed Fletcher

A. _The Enforcer_

B. _Marked Woman_

C. _The Valachi Papers_

D. _The Purple Gang_

E. _The Boss_

4. Independent gangsters or syndicate gangsters who later became too independent were exterminated by the syndicate, many in restaurants. Match the "rubbed-out" independent gangster with the restaurant where he was murdered.

_____ **1.** Willie Moretti

_____ **2.** Joe "The Boss" Masseria

_____ **3.** "Dutch" Schultz

_____ **4.** Joey Gallo

_____ **5.** Jack Zuta

A. Scarpato's Restaurant, Coney Island, New York

B. Lakeview Hotel Restaurant & Dance Hall, Upper Nemahbin Lake, Wisconsin

C. Joe's Restaurant, Cliffside Park, New Jersey

D. Palace Chop House, Newark, New Jersey

E. Umberto's Clam House, New York City

5. Match the Mafia boss in the syndicate with the city he controlled or shared control of with other Mafia members.

_____ **1.** Sam "Momo" Giancana

_____ **2.** Vincent Mangano

_____ **3.** Carlos Marcello

_____ **4.** Raymond Patriarca

_____ **5.** Al Polizzi

_____ **6.** Jack Dragna

A. New York

B. Los Angeles

C. Chicago

D. Providence, Rhode Island

E. New Orleans

F. Cleveland

QUIZ B

The following statements are either true or false. Score 3 points for each correct answer.

1. The largest amounts of money gleaned by today's syndicate stem from the sale of hard drugs. True or False?

2. The formation of the syndicate was really the brainchild of 1920s gangster Angelo Genna. True or False?

3. The formation of the syndicate was really the brainchild of retired 1920s gangster Johnny Torrio. True or False?

4. The so-called Castellammarese War in New York during the early 1930s was really a mopping-up action by young syndicate leaders to eliminate opposition to their authority. True or False?

5. New York syndicate gangster Vito Genovese's right-hand man was Tony Bender, alias Anthony Strollo. True or False?

6. Chicago's Frank Nitti, who inherited Al Capone's mantle with respect to the Chicago "family" and was the syndicate chieftain of the Midwest, committed suicide rather than go to jail in 1943. True or False?

7. Willie Bioff was the syndicate's national boss of the linen-supply business; he retired to Hot Springs with millions and died in bed. True or False?

8. Carmine Galante, a Mafia don and syndicate chieftain, never left Palermo, Sicily, but ruled the American syndicate from abroad. True or False?

9. "Uncle Frank" was a sobriquet for Frank Nitti. True or False?

10. Banished syndicate chieftain Lucky Luciano sneaked into Cuba in 1947 to meet secretly with leaders to plan the syndicate's postwar strategy. True or False?

QUIZ C

Score 4 points for each correct answer.

1. Only one board member of the syndicate was ever executed, electrocuted for murder in Sing Sing in 1944. Who was he?

_____ **A.** Louis Buchalter

_____ **B.** Vito Genovese

_____ **C.** Stefano Magaddino

2. Two lieutenants of the above-mentioned syndicate board member were sent to the electric chair with him. Who were they?

_____ **A.** Bo Weinberg

_____ **B.** Mendy Weiss

_____ **C.** Joey Rao

_____ **D.** Louis Capone

3. The syndicate attempted to control Hollywood through extortion in the late 1930s. Who were the two men assigned to strong-arm the movie moguls?

_____ **A.** Frank "Chew Tobacco" Ryan

_____ **B.** Willie Bioff

_____ **C.** Walter Sage

_____ **D.** George E. Browne

_____ **E.** Anthony Russo

4. In syndicate argot, what term is synonymous with a killing?

_____ **A.** Contract

_____ **B.** Hit

_____ **C.** Bump

_____ **D.** All of the above

5. Which Old World criminal organizations provided the nucleus for the newborn syndicate?

_____ **A.** The Black Hand

_____ **B.** The Mafia

_____ **C.** La Cosa Nostra

_____ **D.** The Camorra

_____ **E.** Unione Siciliane

6. What film used the words "the syndicate" for the first time in motion pictures?

_____ **A.** *Lights of New York*

_____ **B.** *Gangs of Chicago*

_____ **C.** *The Gangster*

7. What syndicate leader headed the sinister "Murder, Inc.," the troop of killers-for-hire, during the 1930s and 1940s?

_____ **A.** Ignazio Saietta

_____ **B.** Joseph Lupo

_____ **C.** Louis Buchalter

8. Who was the chief informer against Murder, Inc., a member of the organization who later "fell" to his death from a window of the Half-Moon Hotel in Coney Island while under heavy police guard?

_____ **A.** "Blue-Jaw" Magoon

_____ **B.** "Dandy Phil" Kastel

_____ **C.** Abe "Kid Twist" Reles

9. Who was the most dedicated killer of Murder, Inc.?

_____ **A.** "Pittsburgh Phil" Strauss

_____ **B.** "Happy" Maione

_____ **C.** "Pretty" Levine

_____ **D.** Mickey "The Louse" Cohen

10. What suave member of the New York syndicate did George Raft pattern his acting manner after?

_____ **A.** Albert Anastasia

_____ **B.** Joe Adonis

_____ **C.** Lucky Luciano

QUIZ D

Match the syndicate member with his profile. Score 5 points for each correct answer.

1. Albert Anastasia
2. Charles Luciano
3. Louis Buchalter
4. Meyer Lansky
5. Vito Genovese

6. Thomas Lucchese
7. Carmine Galante
8. John Roselli
9. Tony Accardo
10. Benjamin Siegel

_____ **A.** A West Coast thug who worked his way up the underworld ladder, he emerged with great power during the late 1960s, but he disappeared in the following decade after allegedly providing federal authorities with important information on the syndicate.

_____ **B.** Called "The Mad Hatter," he would kill people if he didn't like their looks. Hearing that a New York resident, Arnold Schuster, had identified the much wanted bank robber Willie "The Actor" Sutton, he ordered Schuster murdered, screaming: "I can't stand squealers!"

_____ **C.** He began by terrorizing union leaders in New York, taking over the garment union, among others, as he steadily rose to be one of the founding fathers of the syndicate.

_____ **D.** A low-profile killer, he eventually took over one of the five Mafia families in New York City. He was known as "Three Fingers Brown," but, as Joe Valachi snorted, "nobody ever called him that to his face." He died of natural causes in 1967.

_____ **E.** Murdering his way to the top of Masseria's gang, he became one of the founding fathers of the syndicate, concentrating on narcotics and prostitution, the latter controlled nation-wide by him by 1933. After serving a prison term he was paroled (supposedly because of the expert information he provided the Allies on the invasion of Sicily) and was then deported in 1946. He was really the "Boss of Bosses" of the syndicate until his death in 1962.

_____ **F.** During his days as a top Capone gunner he was called "Joe Batters" because he used a baseball bat on victims. He rose to become the reigning syndicate boss of Chicago.

_____ **G.** A ruthless killer, he was known as "Lillo" and "The Cigar." His first offense, in 1921, at the age of eleven, brought him a juvenile sentence for assault and battery. By the 1930s, he was holding up trolley cars. Later he worked for Vito Genovese as an enforcer. He is credited with the murder of Carlos Tresca, an anti-Fascist New York editor. He became an underboss to Joseph Bonanno and, after serving a long prison term for drug smuggling, was released to briefly take over the New York position of "Boss of Bosses" during the late 1970s. He was murdered in 1979, a cigar clenched in his teeth.

_____ **H.** He is credited with killing at least twenty men in the New York rackets wars before being sent to the West Coast to open up drug smuggling and gambling for the syndicate. He was murdered in the Beverly Hills home of his girlfriend, Virginia Hill, in 1947 as he sat reading the *Los Angeles Times.*

_____ **I.** Perhaps the most sinister of all the early-day syndicate members, he worked as underboss to Charles Luciano, making his millions in drugs. He fled the U.S. in 1934 to escape a murder charge (he was named as a killer by one of his own enforcers, Ernest "The Hawk" Rupolo). He lived in Italy and worked for Mussolini, returning to the U.S. in 1946. He became the boss of the Luciano family after bullying Frank Costello to the sidelines. He was sent to prison for a narcotics conspiracy, but controlled his "family" from prison until dying in a Leavenworth cell in 1969.

_____ **J.** They called him "The Genius" because of his uncanny business sense. This founding father of the syndicate spent most of his time behind the scenes, pulling strings for Luciano, concentrating on syndicate investments such as Cuban gambling casinos during the Batista era. He fled to Israel but was deported back to the U.S. as undesirable. He is living out his life in so-called retirement at this writing.

SCORING

Quiz A _____

Quiz B _____

Quiz C _____

Quiz D _____

Chapter Total Score _____

Your Mob Squad Rating

If you scored between 292 and 216	You should head the next Senate hearing on organized crime.
If you scored between 215 and 86	You can spot most of the "boys" on sight.
If you scored between 85 and 0	Transfer to Missing Persons.

WOMEN

IN

CRIME

WOMEN

IN

CRIME

The most provocative, sometimes insidious, always fascinating miscreants are the criminals with the feminine touch. As a killer, the female has proved much more sinister than the male over the centuries, generally preferring to slowly poison her victim to death. The female as con artist has been an even craftier creature than her male counterpart, for in addition to her intricate scams she has cleverly used her sex to achieve her ends. Even as pirates, bandits, and burglars, females have consistently been a nerveless, steel-minded lot, obsessed not with enacting the crime itself, as is the case with the male, but with completing it tidily.

The reader will no doubt recall the women criminals in the following quizzes as the familiar names leap forward, just as they did from newspaper headlines and in motion pictures and televison. Good luck with the ladies.

QUIZ A

Score 5 points for each correct answer.

1. Match the aristocratic killer with her native land.

_____	**1.** Lady Frances Howard	**A.**	Hungary
		B.	France
_____	**2.** Countess Maria Tarnowska	**C.**	Germany
_____	**3.** Countess Elizabeth Bathory	**D.**	England
		E.	Russia
_____	**4.** Marquise Marie de Brinvilliers		
_____	**5.** Countess Sophie Ursinus		

2. Match the criminal with her male partner.

_____	**1.** Bonnie Parker	**A.**	Carl Austin Hall
_____	**2.** "Chicago May" Churchill	**B.**	Raymond Fernandez
_____	**3.** Martha Beck	**C.**	Clyde Barrow
_____	**4.** Bonnie Heady	**D.**	The Sundance Kid
_____	**5.** Etta Place	**E.**	Eddie Guerin

3. Match the mass poisoner with her native land.

_____	**1.** La Voisin	**A.**	Germany
_____	**2.** Jane Toppan	**B.**	United States
_____	**3.** La Toffania	**C.**	Spain
_____	**4.** Helen Jagado	**D.**	Italy
_____	**5.** Christa Lehmann	**E.**	France

4. Match the killer with her murder weapon.

_____	**1.** Kate Bender	**A.**	Poison
_____	**2.** Mrs. Edith Carew	**B.**	Ax
_____	**3.** Ruth Snyder	**C.**	Knife
_____	**4.** Dr. Alice Wynekoop	**D.**	Sash weight
_____	**5.** Maria Barberi	**E.**	Gun

5. Match the criminal with her sobriquet.

_____	**1.** Ruth Synder	**A.**	"The Veiled Murderess"
_____	**2.** Martha Beck	**B.**	"The Lonely Hearts Killer"
_____	**3.** Clara Phillips	**C.**	"The Tiger Woman"
_____	**4.** Lydia Sherman	**D.**	"The Angel-Maker"
_____	**5.** Mrs. Julius Fazekas	**E.**	"The Granite Woman"
_____	**6.** Henrietta Robinson	**F.**	"Queen Poisoner"
_____	**7.** Louise Rolfe	**G.**	"The Bandit Queen"
_____	**8.** Ella Watson	**H.**	"The Blonde Alibi"
_____	**9.** Winnie Ruth Judd	**I.**	"Cattle Kate"
_____	**10.** Belle Starr	**J.**	"The Trunk Murderess"

6. Match the killer with her native state.

_____	**1.** Louise Peete	**A.**	Kansas
_____	**2.** Alice Crimmins	**B.**	New York
_____	**3.** Patty Columbo	**C.**	Oklahoma
_____	**4.** Belle Gunness	**D.**	California
_____	**5.** Kate Bender	**E.**	Indiana
_____	**6.** Nannie Doss	**F.**	Illinois

7. Match the true-life criminal with the movie star and motion picture profiling her life.

_____ **1.** Bonnie Parker

_____ **2.** Barbara Graham

_____ **3.** Virginia Hill

_____ **4.** "Ma" Barker

_____ **5.** Anne Bonny

A. Maureen O'Hara in *Against All Flags*

B. Shelley Winters in *Bloody Mama*

C. Joan Crawford in *The Damned Don't Cry*

D. Sylvia Sidney in *You Only Live Once*

E. Susan Hayward in *I Want to Live*

8. Match the gun moll with her gangster lover.

_____	**1.** Evelyn Frechette	**A.**	"Big Jim" Colosimo
_____	**2.** Dale Winter	**B.**	Volney Davis
_____	**3.** Edna Murray	**C.**	John Dillinger
_____	**4.** Marion "Kiki" Roberts	**D.**	"Machine Gun" Jack McGurn
_____	**5.** Louise Rolfe	**E.**	Jack Diamond

QUIZ B

The following statements are either true or false. Score 3 points for each correct answer.

1. The first woman executed by hanging in the United States was Ruth Ellis.   True or False?

2. "Ma" Barker was distantly related to Frank and Jesse James.   True or False?

3. Polly Adler and the Everleigh Sisters were brothel madams.   True or False?

4. The all-time mass murderer among female killers was Mother Needham of England.   True or False?

5. Ruth Synder, who was executed for the murder of her husband in 1928, was photographed dying in Sing Sing's electric chair.   True or False?

6. Margie Dean and Cecelia Cooney were both armed bandits of the 1920s.   True or False?

7. Amy Archer-Gilligan and Dorothea Waddingham were nurses in the United States and England who murdered their patients.   True or False?

8. Nannie Doss of Oklahoma was a notorious fence.   True or False?

9. Bella Anderson was the first American female kidnapper.   True or False?

10. Mary Blandy, executed in England while wearing a dress, told the executioner: "For decency's sake, don't hang me high."   True or False?

QUIZ C

Score 4 points for each correct answer.

1. Who was the first American female pirate?

    _____ **A.** Penny Bjorkland

    _____ **B.** Jane Swett

    _____ **C.** Anne Bonny

2. Which among the following female killers was a successful novelist?

    _____ **A.** Hera Myrtel

    _____ **B.** Jane Housden

    _____ **C.** Catherine Wilson

3. Hanged for stealing in 1763 in England, which of the following female criminals battled the executioner and actually hanged herself?

    _____ **A.** Elizabeth Grieve

    _____ **B.** Hannah Dagoe

    _____ **C.** Barbara Spencer

4. Which female swindler practiced spiritualism scams, calling herself "The Swami"?

    _____ **A.** Sophie Bluffstein

    _____ **B.** Cassie Chadwick

    _____ **C.** Edith Solomon

5. Which female swindler was still "compromising" men in her eighties?

   _____ **A.** Ellen Peck

   _____ **B.** Martha Marek

   _____ **C.** Mildred Hill

6. Select the two women who attempted to assassinate President Gerald Ford.

   _____ **A.** Denise Labbe

   _____ **B.** Sarah Jane Moore

   _____ **C.** Constance Kent

   _____ **D.** Mary Moders

   _____ **E.** Lynette Fromme

7. Which of the following were part of Charles Manson's grotesque murder cult in southern California?

   _____ **A.** Leslie Van Houten

   _____ **B.** Patricia Krenwinkel

   _____ **C.** Fredericka Mandelbaum

   _____ **D.** Susan Atkins

   _____ **E.** All of the above

8. Select the notorious female pickpocket immortalized in *The Threepenny Opera*.

   _____ **A.** Mary Bateman

   _____ **B.** Catherine Hayes

   _____ **C.** Jenny Diver

9. Who was the Massachusetts spinster who allegedly

> *— took an ax*
> *And gave her mother forty whacks;*
> *When she saw what she had done*
> *She gave her father forty-one.*

_____ **A.** Marie de Brinvilliers

_____ **B.** Lizzie Borden

_____ **C.** Elizabeth Mason

10. What female bandit of the early 1930s penned a crude poem called "Suicide Sal," which was later widely published in newspapers?

_____ **A.** Mary Ann Cotton

_____ **B.** Pamela Lee Worms

_____ **C.** Bonnie Parker

QUIZ D

Match the criminal with her profile. Score 5 points for each correct answer.

1. Bonnie Parker
2. "Ma" Barker
3. Marie de Brinvilliers
4. Kathryn Kelly
5. Moll Cutpurse

6. Cecelia Cooney
7. Priscilla Bradford
8. Irma Grese
9. Cassie Chadwick
10. Jenny Diver

_____ **A.** A Brooklyn laundress, she turned to holdups with her husband to provide a nest egg for their unborn child. She robbed wildly in Brooklyn during the early 1920s and was known across the nation as "The Bobbed-Haired Bandit."

_____ **B.** Celebrated in song and story, she was England's most notorious pickpocket, a woman who made a fortune with her nimble fingers but found it impossible to retire with her riches — a flaw which caused her execution.

_____ **C.** She began as a West Coast prostitute, migrating to Canada and then to Ohio, where she married an unsuspecting doctor. She busied herself with petty con games, then hit upon the idea of passing herself off as the illegitimate daughter of Andrew Carnegie, a scheme that brought her millions before she was exposed and sent to prison.

_____ **D.** Born in Texas, she met her bandit lover when she was a waitress and immediately embarked on a crime spree, robbing and killing her way through the Southwest before she and her murderous companion were shot to pieces by a posse in 1934.

_____ **E.** A youthful ogre whose unbridled sadism and sexual perversion caused the deaths of hundreds if not thousands of helpless prisoners, she was executed in 1945 as a German war criminal.

_____ **F.** She preferred the clothes of the male, shocking seventeenth-century England. She was unquestionably the world's first great female criminal of record, who amassed a fortune through fencing, pickpocketing, blackmail, and highway robbery.

_____ **G.** This criminal harridan raised a brood of killer sons, whose bank robbing and kidnapping in the 1930s she helped to plan. She and her youngest son, Freddie, were killed in a wild shoot-out with FBI agents at Lake Weir, Florida, in 1935.

_____ **H.** She promoted the image of her husband as a fierce bank robber and kidnapper who would not hesitate to kill with a machine gun to accomplish his ends. She was the actual brains behind her husband's crimes, a beautiful and uncompromising woman of great nerve and daring, who smiled winningly for the cameras as she was sent to prison for life for kidnapping Oklahoma oil man Charles Urschel.

_____ **I.** A mass poisoner, this aristocratic female murdered her father, other relatives, and anyone else who displeased her. She poisoned scores of patients in a hospital merely to determine the effectiveness of new poisons. She was finally apprehended and executed, but not before killing at least 100 people.

_____ **J.** A middle-class American housewife, she and two friends brutally killed her husband in 1980 in Florida so that his business, according to the confession of one of the killers, could become an "all-female" operation.

SCORING

Quiz A   _____

Quiz B   _____

Quiz C   _____

Quiz D   _____

    Chapter Total Score   _____

Your Female Division Rating

If you scored between 362 and 271

You are a match for any Moll Cutpurse.

If you scored between 270 and 86

Your intuition is good but study is needed.

If you scored between 85 and 0

Go back to the training academy.

SOLUTIONS

SOLUTIONS

ASSASSINS

Quiz A

1. 1. B   2. E   3. D   4. A   5. C

2. 1. D   2. C   3. E   4. A   5. B

3. 1. B   2. E   3. A   4. C   5. D

4. 1. C   2. A   3. B   4. E   5. D

5. 1. E   2. C   3. D   4. B   5. A

6. 1. D   2. F   3. B   4. C   5. A   6. E

Quiz B

1. False. Booth thought he was ridding the world of a despot.   **2.** True   **3.** True. Catherine's act was one of self-preservation since she knew she was on Peter's murder list.   **4.** False. Messalina cheated on Claudius and he had her executed; it was his fourth wife, Agrippina, who poisoned him.   **5.** True. Becket would not lift his excommunications of dissolute nobles, which enraged Henry II, who was behind the clergyman's assassination.   **6.** True   **7.** False. Oswald was shot and killed by Jack Ruby on November 24, 1964.   **8.** False. Sirhan was a Palestinian, whose motive remains unclear to this day.   **9.** True   **10.** True   **11.** True   **12.** False. Julius Caesar was killed on that date.   **13.** True   **14.** True, but he later retracted the confession.   **15.** True

Quiz C

1. B	2. C	3. C	4. A	5. B
6. C	7. A	8. A	9. C	10. A

Quiz D

1. C	2. E	3. G	4. B	5. I
6. A	7. J	8. D	9. F	10. H

CON ARTISTS

Quiz A

1.	1. D	2. C	3. B	4. E	5. A
2.	1. B	2. D	3. A	4. E	5. C
3.	1. B	2. E	3. D	4. C	5. A
4.	1. D	2. C	3. E	4. A	5. B
5.	1. C	2. E	3. B	4. D	5. A

Quiz B

1. True **2.** True **3.** True; several French government officials were implicated in Stavisky's bond-selling schemes. **4.** False, though Fisk reportedly entertained Grant during a crucial period when he was trying to corner the gold market with his friend Jay Gould, distracting the President's attention from their operations. **5.** True **6.** False. The inside man is the operator of the con game. **7.** True **8.** False. Mizener was Jolson's friend. **9.** True **10.** True. Benny was only one of many Hollywood stars who were bilked in this gigantic swindle.

Quiz C

1. B	2. B	3. A	4. C	5. B
6. A	7. B	8. C	9. B	10. C

Quiz D

1. D	**2.** B	**3.** M	**4.** K	**5.** C
6. H	**7.** N	**8.** L	**9.** I	**10.** G
11. J	**12.** O	**13.** E	**14.** A	**15.** F

GANGS AND GANGSTERS

Quiz A

1. 1. E	2. D	3. A	4. B	5. C
2. 1. B	2. C	3. A	4. E	5. D
3. 1. C	2. A	3. D	4. E	5. B
4. 1. C	2. B	3. A	4. E	5. D
5. 1. C	2. A	3. B	4. E	5. D
6. 1. B	2. C	3. E	4. A	5. D
7. 1. B	2. A	3. D	4. E	5. C
8. 1. E	2. C	3. D	4. B	5. A
9. 1. A	2. C	3. B	4. E	5. D
10. 1. B	2. A	3. D	4. E	5. C
11. 1. D	2. E	3. G	4. F	5. A
6. C	7. B			
12. 1. B	2. E	3. A	4. F	5. G
6. D	7. C			
13. 1. D	2. E	3. F	4. A	5. I
6. G	7. C	8. B	9. H	
14. 1. D	2. C	3. B	4. E	5. A
15. 1. E	2. D	3. F	4. B	5. C
6. A				

Quiz B

1. False. The scars were on the left side of his face.   **2.** True
3. True   **4.** True   **5.** False. Esposito was a lesser ally.
6. True   **7.** True   **8.** False. They were mortal enemies;
the Gennas worked for Capone.   **9.** True   **10.** True

Quiz C

1. C   **2.** B   **3.** A (Saltisville, no longer extant)   **4.** B
5. B   **6.** C   **7.** A   **8.** C   **9.** A   **10.** B

Quiz D

1. J   **2.** B   **3.** G   **4.** D   **5.** E
6. C   **7.** H   **8.** F   **9.** I   **10.** A

THE KIDNAPPERS

Quiz A

1. 1. C   2. F   3. A   4. E   5. D
    6. B

2. 1. B   2. E   3. C   4. A   5. D

3. 1. D   2. E   3. C   4. B   5. A

4. 1. D   2. C   3. B   4. A   5. E

5. 1. A   2. B   3. E   4. C   5. D

Quiz B

1. True   **2.** True, in 1874   **3.** False   **4.** True. The ransom was eventually paid and Richard was released.   **5.** True **6.** False. He was released unharmed.   **7.** False. Hickman murdered the child and was executed for the crime. **8.** True **9.** True   **10.** True. They went to death together, strapped into two chairs in the gas chamber.

Quiz C

1. B	**2.** C	**3.** B	**4.** A	**5.** B
6. C	**7.** A	**8.** A	**9.** C	**10.** B

Quiz D

1. I	**2.** H	**3.** J	**4.** C	**5.** D
6. A	**7.** G	**8.** B	**9.** F	**10.** E

THE KILLERS

Quiz A

1.	1. D	2. C	3. B	4. A	5. E
2.	1. F	2. J	3. I	4. B	5. D
	6. A	7. C	8. H	9. E	10. G
3.	1. I	2. G	3. D	4. H	5. J
	6. F	7. C	8. E	9. A	10. B
4.	1. B	2. E	3. C	4. A	5. D
5.	1. C	2. E	3. D	4. A	5. B

6. 1. B   2. E   3. D   4. A   5. C

7. 1. G   2. A   3. D   4. E   5. C
      6. B   7. F

8. 1. F   2. E   3. H   4. A   5. D
      6. B   7. C   8. G   9. J   10. I

9. 1. I   2. D   3. F   4. B   5. C
      6. E   7. A   8. G   9. H

10. 1. E   2. I   3. J   4. A   5. C
       6. B   7. F   8. G   9. H   10. D

Quiz B

1. True   **2.** True   **3.** False. Hoch married and murdered spinsters.   **4.** True   **5.** True   **6.** True   **7.** False. Nash was a victim, along with his crew; his mate, Bram, was pinpointed as the killer.   **8.** False. Payne planted a bomb in the family car to murder his wife.   **9.** True   **10.** False. Mrs. Beck was as guilty as Fernandez.   **11.** False. Greenlease was killed in Kansas.   **12.** True   **13.** False. Cowan was brooding over being fired.   **14.** True   **15.** True   **16.** True   **17.** False. Holmes, who indeed was America's all-time mass murderer, was a pharmacist.   **18.** True. Gacy was photographed shaking the First Lady's hand at a political rally; he was a Democratic precinct worker.   **19.** False   **20.** True

Quiz C

1. A   **2.** C   **3.** A   **4.** B   **5.** C
6. B   **7.** C   **8.** B   **9.** C   **10.** A
11. C   **12.** A   **13.** B   **14.** B   **15.** A
16. A   **17.** B   **18.** C   **19.** B   **20.** A

Quiz D

1. D   **2.** G   **3.** N   **4.** S   **5.** H
6. E   **7.** L   **8.** R   **9.** T   **10.** I
11. O   **12.** P   **13.** F   **14.** A   **15.** M
16. J   **17.** K   **18.** Q   **19.** C   **20.** B

THE LAWMEN

Quiz A

1. 1. C   2. D   3. B   4. A   5. F
6. E

2. 1. E   2. A   3. D   4. C   5. B

3. 1. E   2. C   3. B   4. A   5. D

4. 1. C   2. E   3. B   4. A   5. D

5. 1. B   2. C   3. E   4. A   5. D

Quiz B

1. True   **2.** False. Cowley was killed in a shoot-out with "Baby-Face" Nelson in 1934; he and another agent had mortally wounded Nelson.   **3.** True   **4.** False. Nelson killed only one agent, named Baum.   **5.** True, to prove that he could make a personal arrest, though FBI agents with drawn guns completely surrounded Karpis as, unarmed, he got out of a car in New Orleans and Hoover stepped forward to make the collar.   **6.** True   **7.** True   **8.** False   **9.** True   **10.** True

Quiz C

1. A   **2.** B   **3.** A   **4.** B   **5.** C
6. B   **7.** C   **8.** A   **9.** C   **10.** B

Quiz D

1. E   **2.** A   **3.** G   **4.** F   **5.** H
6. J   **7.** D   **8.** I   **9.** C   **10.** B

MOUTHPIECES

Quiz A

1. 1. B   2. E   3. A   4. C   5. D

2. 1. E   2. C   3. F   4. A   5. B
   6. D

3. 1. B   2. A   3. D   4. E   5. C

4. 1. B   2. A   3. D   4. C

5. 1. B   2. A   3. E   4. C   5. D

Quiz B

1. True. The case against Darrow was dismissed.   **2.** True
3. False. Darrow's offices were in Chicago.   **4.** True
5. True   **6.** False. The phrase means literally "the body or substance of the crime or offense," not the corpse.   **7.** True
8. True   **9.** False. Maine was the first state, in 1864.
10. False. Fallon did not drink in court, but managed to put away a great deal of alcohol outside the chambers where he practiced. He had no great love for Rothstein.

Quiz C

1. A   **2.** B   **3.** A   **4.** C   **5.** B
6. C   **7.** A   **8.** A   **9.** C   **10.** C

Quiz D

1. D   **2.** A   **3.** E   **4.** B   **5.** C

THE OUTLAWS

Quiz A

1. 1. B   2. C   3. D   4. A   5. H
6. E   7. F   8. G

2. 1. D   2. C   3. B   4. E   5. A

3. 1. J   2. I   3. H   4. G   5. F
6. E   7. D   8. C   9. B   10. A

4. 1. D   2. A   3. B   4. E   5. C

5. 1. B   2. E   3. D   4. F   5. C
6. A

6. 1. F   2. A   3. B   4. E   5. D
6. C

7. 1. B   2. C   3. A   4. E   5. D

Quiz B
1. True   **2.** False. The Buck Gang terrorized Oklahoma.
3. False. Jesse James, from all worthwhile accounts, was a cold-blooded murderer.   **4.** True   **5.** True   **6.** False. Jim went to prison and Rube was killed by a railway guard. **7.** False. Jennings was the most inept bandit in Western history, his total take not more than a thousand dollars. **8.** False. Grat was killed along with Bob Dalton; Emmett Dalton survived.   **9.** True   **10.** True

Quiz C
1. C   **2.** D   **3.** C   **4.** B   **5.** A
6. A   **7.** D   **8.** C   **9.** A   **10.** A, B
and C

Quiz D
1. B   **2.** H   **3.** C   **4.** J   **5.** I
6. F   **7.** E   **8.** D   **9.** A   **10.** G

PRISONS AND PRISONERS

Quiz A

1. 1. E   2. D   3. A   4. C   5. B

2. 1. B   2. A   3. E   4. C   5. D

3. 1. D   2. A   3. B   4. E   5. C

4. 1. E   2. C   3. B   4. A   5. D

5. 1. B   2. E   3. A   4. C   5. D

6. 1. C   2. A   3. B   4. D   5. E

Quiz B

1. True   **2.** True. Dillinger carved the crude gun from the top of a washboard and blackened it with boot polish; he later posed smilingly with the wooden gun outside his father's Indiana farmhouse.   **3.** True   **4.** False. Landru made no attempt to escape; if he had, he would never have returned, according to his nature.   **5.** False. The escape of Ralph Roe and Theodore "Sunny" Cole in 1935 may have been successful (their bodies were never found; the authorities claimed they had drowned), as was the clever escape from Alcatraz by Frank Lee Morris and Clarence and Joseph Anglin in 1962.   **6.** False. Stroud experimented with cures for birds.   **7.** True   **8.** True   **9.** True   **10.** False, but the metal in Fish's body did cause great clouds of blue smoke to rise from his electrified body.

Quiz C

1. B   **2.** C   **3.** C   **4.** B   **5.** B
6. C   **7.** D   **8.** C   **9.** D   **10.** A

Quiz D

1. D   **2.** A   **3.** H   **4.** J   **5.** E
6. C   **7.** I   **8.** B   **9.** G   **10.** F

THE SYNDICATE

Quiz A

1. 1. D 2. C 3. F 4. A 5. B
6. E

2. 1. I 2. H 3. B 4. J 5. G
6. C 7. F 8. E 9. D 10. A

3. 1. C 2. A 3. B 4. E 5. D

4. 1. C 2. A 3. D 4. E 5. B

5. 1. C 2. A 3. E 4. D 5. F
6. B

Quiz B

1. True. Some estimates range above $1 billion a year.
2. False. Genna was a Capone flunky. **3.** True. Torrio sold the idea to Luciano, Lansky, and others in New York when he went into supposed "retirement" in the late 1920s. **4.** False. This was an East Coast gang war between Masseria and Maranzano, Mafia dons termed "Moustache Petes" by those who later formed the syndicate. **5.** True **6.** True
7. False. Bioff and his partner, George Browne, extorted from Hollywood moguls on orders from the syndicate. Bioff absconded with money, then turned informer, for which he was later murdered. **8.** False. Galante was briefly the "boss of bosses" in New York, until his extermination by rivals in 1979. **9.** False. "Uncle Frank" was New York syndicate chieftain Frank Costello. **10.** True

Quiz C

1. A **2.** B and D **3.** B and D **4.** D **5.** B and C
(The latter was strictly an East Coast version of the Mafia.)
6. C **7.** C **8.** C **9.** A **10.** B (Adonis was Raft's friend before Raft became a professional escort and dancer and then went to Hollywood to play tough guys.)

Quiz D

1. B	**2.** E	**3.** C	**4.** J	**5.** I
6. D	**7.** G	**8.** A	**9.** F	**10.** H

WOMEN IN CRIME

Quiz A

1. 1. D	2. E	3. A	4. B	5. C
2. 1. C	2. E	3. B	4. A	5. D
3. 1. E	2. B	3. D	4. C	5. A
4. 1. B	2. A	3. D	4. E	5. C
5. 1. E	2. B	3. C	4. F	5. D
6. A	7. H	8. I	9. J	10. G
6. 1. D	2. B	3. F	4. E	5. A
6. C				
7. 1. D	2. E	3. C	4. B	5. A
8. 1. C	2. A	3. B	4. E	5. D

Quiz B

1. False. Ruth Ellis was the last woman hanged in England (for murder); the first woman hanged in the United States was Mary Surratt, after being summarily convicted in the Lincoln conspiracy in 1865. **2.** True **3.** True **4.** False— Mother Needham was a procuress. The all-time mass murderer among females to this date is undoubtedly the mad Hungarian countess Elizabeth Bathory, credited with killing

610 peasant girls. **5.** True **6.** True **7.** True **8.** False. Nannie murdered at least a dozen people, poisoning most of her family, and especially husbands, in her search for "the perfect romance." **9.** True. Bella Anderson kidnapped twenty-month-old Marion Clarke from her New York home in May 1899; the child was later returned and Anderson was given a four-year term. **10.** True

Quiz C
1. C **2.** A **3.** B **4.** C **5.** A **6.** B and E
7. A, B, and D **8.** C **9.** B **10.** C

Quiz D
1. D **2.** G **3.** I **4.** H **5.** F
6. A **7.** J **8.** E **9.** C **10.** B

FINAL SCORING

Assassins   _____

Con Artists   _____

Gangs and Gangsters   _____

The Kidnappers   _____

The Killers   _____

The Lawmen   _____

Mouthpieces   _____

The Outlaws   _____

Prisons and Prisoners   _____

The Syndicate   _____

Women in Crime   _____

    Book Total Score   _____

Your Overall Rating as a Sleuth of True Crime

If your overall score is between 3,535 and 2,592

Your badge is gold and is pinned in the Hall of Fame.

If your overall score is between 2,591 and 1,032

Your silver badge will blind any criminal.

If your overall score is between 1,031 and 0

Be cautious in showing your credentials; you may be arrested for impersonating an officer.